THE MARSHALL CAVENDISH
☆ ☆ ☆ ILLUSTRATED ☆ ☆ ☆
ENCYCLOPEDIA OF
WORLD WAR II

VOLUME 23

THE MARSHALL CAVENDISH
☆ ☆ ☆ ILLUSTRATED ☆ ☆ ☆
ENCYCLOPEDIA OF
WORLD WAR II

Based on the original text by
Lieutenant Colonel Eddy Bauer

CONSULTANT EDITOR

Brigadier General James L. Collins, Jr., U.S.A.
CHIEF OF MILITARY HISTORY, DEPARTMENT OF THE ARMY

MARSHALL CAVENDISH CORPORATION/NEW YORK

CONTENTS

Editorial Director: Brian Innes
Editor-in-chief; Brigadier Peter Young, D.S.O., M.C., M.A.
Managing Editor: Richard Humble
Editor: Christopher Chant
Art Editor: Jim Bridge

The War Artists

Leonard Rosoman

E. GABAIN

Soon after the outbreak of war, the War Artists scheme, which had proved so successful towards the end of World War I, was revived in Britain. Certainly in the first two years of the war it had remarkable results as painters and sculptors found new subjects to study which, at the same time, satisfied their feelings of patriotism and the community spirit throughout the country.
Page 3081: "A House Collapsing on Two Firemen, Shoe Lane, London, E.C.4." by Leonard Rosoman, A.R.A. This oil painting, of a scene that was all too familiar during the Blitz, points up how an artist could often capture the drama of a moment that a photographer might miss altogether.
△◁ "We Can Take It" by Ruskin Spear. This watercolour, executed at the height of the Blitz, evokes perfectly the spirit of Londoners in the dark days of 1940-41.
▽◁ "Sandbag Filling" by Ethel Gabain. One of the few women working within the War Artists scheme, Ethel Gabain concentrated on using women and children at work for her subjects, as in this lithograph set in Islington.
◁ "St. Bride's and the City After the Fire" on December 29, 1940 – a chalk and pen sketch of one of London's favourite churches after it was hit by German bombs. This is just one of many works by Sir Muirhead Bone under the sponsorship of the W.A.A.C.

△◁ L. S. Lowry's "Going to Work", an oil painted in 1943. As one of the few English painters who deliberately turned his back on London, Lowry's work is unique in its studies of northern towns, factories, and workers.

▽◁ A watercolour of a Sunderland flying boat being serviced, by Norman Wilkinson, C.B.E.

△ One of a series of 136 working sketches in pencil by Sir Stanley Spencer, R.A., preparatory to his "Shipbuilding on the Clyde" paintings. One of the most original of English painters, Spencer turned from his more usual rural subjects to this industrial study with an enthusiasm which demonstrates itself in the final work.

◁ Part of the finished work–the centre panel of the section entitled "Burners".

3085

3086

One of Britain's most distinguished sculptors, Henry Moore, was an Official War Artist between 1940 and 1942. It is perhaps surprising that a man famous for his massive sculptures could execute works of such delicate colouring and feeling. These three studies of Londoners patiently waiting through the night in the Underground are in chalk, wash, and ink.
◁◁ "Woman Seated in the Underground".
△ "Pink and Green Sleepers".
◁ "Grey Tube Shelter".
Overleaf: "On the Strip-Line" by Terence Cuneo. This conté and chalk drawing of Churchill tanks being dismantled brings home the ordered chaos of a huge assembly shop.

3088

The greatest – or best known – war paintings of all are Goya's works during the Peninsular War, and Picasso's "Guernica", which he painted during the Spanish Civil War. War painters, particularly official ones, were not sadistic in what they portrayed. Their job was to record and report, and Great Britain was fortunate that the War Artists' Advisory Committee organised exhibitions around the smaller galleries in the country as well as the National Galleries in cities.

When war was declared, the War Artists' Advisory Committee recommended the government to appoint war artists to work for the Admiralty, the War Office, and the Air Ministry, and others to have roving commissions, following the war around. Several of the original World War I artists were immediately appointed – Sir Muirhead Bone, the Nash brothers John and Paul, Eric Kennington, Charles Cundall, William Roberts, and Henry Lamb.

After the experiences with equipment during World War I, the painters were encouraged to use "easy" media, such as water colours, crayon, and pencil. The bulk and slowness of oil painting equipment and its results meant that oils were unsuitable for purely journalistic paintings, though many people did large oil canvases later.

Public interest was keen; even as early as 1940, two exhibitions of war paintings were held in the National Gallery in London (the Old Masters and the other collections at the gallery had been dispersed all over the country for safety in case the gallery was bombed). It was the first time that modern paintings had ever been shown in the National Gallery; every month new pictures were added to the exhibition. The thirst needed slaking; with the background of the war pictures, famous musicians played at lunchtime concerts, always packed.

The Royal Academy was also able to help the War Artists; in 1940 an exhibition was staged there for the Red Cross and Artists General Benevolent Fund. Although four of the galleries at the Academy had been burnt out and were unusable because of bombs, several exhibitions were held there – the two most famous being a collection of poster designs by children, and one of paintings by the "firemen" artists.

For the duration of the war, the National Portrait Gallery housed and displayed the work of men in the armed forces – the collection there had also been dispersed because of the danger of them being burnt or blown up. The W.A.A.C. was particularly interested in paintings submitted by serving soldiers. They often had the freshness and vitality of personal involvement which was sometimes lacking in the "official" paintings.

The Civil Defence, seemingly an unlikely source of war pictures, had started in 1941 to band together to hold exhibitions of its members' paintings, particularly of their work among the "ordinary" people. Many of these pictures were bought by the War Artists' Advisory Committee and were eventually added to the collection of the National Portrait Gallery.

Apart from the actual war artists, there were many other different sorts of painters who contribute to our knowledge of conditions between 1939 and 1945. A number of European Surrealists fled, at the outbreak of war, to the United States, where they continued to work. Max Ernst, who had been banned by the Nazis, was among them and others were Yves Tanguy, Kurt Seligmann,

Lawrence Jacob, George Grosz, and Philip Evergood. Although the effects of the war were cataclysmic in Europe, they spread worldwide to include these painters, whose works show as clearly as a bombed building the horrors, boredom, and discomfort of war.

Women played a vital part in both the world wars in factories and on the land. One of the most famous artists of World War II is Evelyn Dunbar, many of whose pictures were officially commissioned. Among her evocative paintings are pictures of St. Thomas's hospital, a knitting party, people queuing for food, the Red Cross at work, anti-gas clothes and how to put them on, land girls working, and camouflage nets being made by recuperating nurses. Many of her pictures hang in the Imperial War Museum. The women's war effort was also recorded pictorially by Dame Laura Knight, Ethel Gabain, and Doris Zinkeisen.

World War II produced many cartoonists who both wrote and illustrated books, pamphlets, and

continued on p. 3098.

Page 3087 top: *John Piper, one of the dominant Neo-Romantic painters, was particularly noted for his architectural landscapes. He was commissioned to do several works for the W.A.A.C., one of which was this watercolour study "Shelter Experiments, Near Woburn, Bedfordshire".*
Page 3087 bottom: *John Edgar Platt's evocative oil painting, "Convoy Passing the Lizard, Cornwall, 1942".*

One of the most popular of modern artists, Felix Topolski, went to Russia on the first convoy from Britain in September 1941, and recorded many of the sights in his familiar style.
◁◁ *"Aboard a Cruiser"–oiling a destroyer at sea in the Arctic (wash).*
△ *"West of Moscow" (watercolour).*
◁ *"In the White Sea"– convoying No. 151 Wing R.A.F. to Russia (watercolour).*

3092

Anthony Gross, Edward Bawden, R.A., and Edward Ardizzone, A.R.A., were three of the most prolific artists working under the War Artists scheme.

△◁ "Chins at War" by Gross – one of a series of pen and wash drawings under the same title. This one shows a party consisting of the official cameraman, an army observer, the artist himself, and their escort of Hakor Chins.

◁◁ "Liberation and Battle of France" was the umbrella for another series of Gross's pen and wash drawings, including this one of General Montgomery.

△ One of a number of watercolours painted by Bawden in Abyssinia – "Gallabat", showing stretcher bearers of the Royal Garhwal Rifles at the Regimental Aid Post.

◁ "Behind Ruweisat Ridge", one of many watercolours painted by Ardizzone during his time with the army in the desert.

△ *"New Guinea Front" by the Japanese painter Tsuguji Fugita.*
▷ *and* △▷ *Two oil paintings by the American war artist Tom Lea, both under the general title "Peleliu".*
▷▷ *"Follow Me", one of a series of paintings depicting major battles in the history of the U.S. Army, commissioned by that body.*

△ *A vigorous naïve painting in oils by an unknown Indian artist of an "Episode in the Battle of Sailum Vum". It shows the heroic action by Subadar Ram Sarup Singh which gained him the V.C. during the fighting in the Chin Hills, Burma.*
▷ *"Attack on Enemy Airfield on Leyte by the Takachiho paratroop unit" by Kengi Yoshioka. Painted in a rather different style from many other Japanese works, it nevertheless conveys graphically the tension at the moment of landing.*
△▷ *A dramatic incident recalled later by the artist—Tom Lea's "Death of the Wasp", Coral Sea, September 15, 1942.*
▷▷ *Another of Lea's series of paintings of the fighting in the Pacific—"Advance on Peleliu, 1944".*

continued from p. 3091.

posters. Particular favourites among the cartoonists are Bill Maulden, Fougasse, Bruce Bairnsfather, Bert Thomas, and Bernard Partridge.

World War II also saw the advent of comic strips and comic strip books. "Jane", a heroine of the *Daily Mirror,* was a great favourite, partly because she was continually losing her clothes. She was a forces' pin-up, and legend grew that the less Jane wore, the better the Allies' military operations went. Comic books had an enormous circulation partly because of their appeal to people needing relaxation away from home.

The War Artists' Advisory Committee, responsible to the Ministry of Information, enjoyed the right to release from military service any painter they thought could usefully contribute to the reportage of war painting; they exercised this right only in the case of Albert Richards.

The Admiralty had two official painters, Charles Cundall and Richard Eurich, but in many houses and museums are pictures of ships done by the men themselves. William Roberts, Henry Lamb, Henry Carr, Edward Bawden, Rodrigo Moynihan, and Anthony Gross painted for the Army; Anthony Gross also did some fine pictures of the members of the French *maquis,* such as La Compagnie Tito in Callac in 1944. Paul Nash and John Armstrong painted for the R.A.F. War work in factories, shipyards, and so on was recorded by Stanley Spencer, R. V. Pitchforth, Kenneth Rowntree, Leslie Cole, A. R. Thompson, L. S. Lowry, and Duncan Grant.

Charles Ginner and the two "firemen" artists, Leonard Rosoman and Paul Desseau, painted the devastating effects of air raid, fire damage, and bombs. Muirhead Bone and John Piper also painted bombed-out ruins and houses in London and the country. Overseas, four official war artists were sent to Australia to record the South-East Asia war. Britain was particularly fortunate that the government was so quick in reviving the successful World War I experiment of official war artists. It resulted in a great body of work – much of it of a very high artistic standard indeed.

Although there are many grandiose German paintings dating from before the start of the war and in the early part of the war, they are not, for the most part, of any great merit artistically. Naturally enough "official" Germany

Official paintings of the Soviet Union and other Eastern European nations are all too often used as propaganda rather than being considered on their merits as artistic works. Of these four, three are very much in the clearly recognisable "heroic" style.
△ "The Partisan's Mother" by the Soviet painter Kerassimou.
▷ "Enver Hoxha with his Partisan Group"; Hoxha is the present-day Albanian leader.
▷ △ "The German Retreat from Novgorod".
▷▷ The Russian artist Volkhov's interpretation of the "Liberation of Minsk".

did not wish to record the failures of the later years.

Russian paintings of the war are plentiful, but the great majority of them were painted after the war had finished. They are largely intended for propaganda purposes, painted in a "heroic" style, and showing their brave soldiers in the most appalling conditions.

Of all the nations, the French recorded events in their country the most precisely, particularly the fall of Paris; there is a fine collection of war paintings in the *Musée de l'Armée*.

Sir Muirhead Bone was the first British official war artist; during World War II he documented bomb damage in London, and one of his most evocative paintings is of St. Bride's church and the City after the fire on December 29, 1940.

He was principally a water-colour painter and etcher, and it was mainly because of his enthusiasm for the war work of other painters that the magnificent collection of paintings at the Imperial War Museum was formed.

Paul Nash was inevitably chosen as an official artist. He had served–and painted–at the front in 1917. His first war work was for the Air Ministry, and many of his paintings show wrecked aeroplanes, German and British; constantly bedevilled by

continued on p. 3106.

3100

◁◁ *A fine German oil painting of an E-boat at sea.*
△ *"Diving Controls of a Submarine"–a delicate watercolour executed in 1940 by Eric Ravilious, who was later killed on active service as a War Artist.*

◁ *There is both movement and depth in this oil "Destroyer Rescuing Survivors" by Richard Eurich, R.A. Eurich held an honorary captaincy in the Royal Marines.*
Overleaf: "The Campbeltown at St. Nazaire"–a spectacular oil painting by Norman Wilkinson.

HASSANI AIRFIELD·ATHENS

△ *Sharp contrast between the machines of war and pastoral life—"Hassani Airfield, Athens", a pen and wash sketch by Harold Hailstone.*

▷ *Thomas Hennell, presumed killed while on active War Artist service, painted a series of watercolours under the general title "H.M.S. Hunter". This one shows the hangar deck of the aircraft-carrier.*

△▷ *W. T. Rawlinson was fascinated by the radar stations which sprang up around the coast of Britain. In his oil paintings he usually pictures them starkly against the sky, guarding the country against the unseen enemy.*

▷▷ *"Interrogation of Pilots". Mervyn Peake's 1944 oil painting picks out of the surrounding gloom the stark faces of men who have just returned from another raid over enemy territory.*

continued from p. 3099.

asthma from 1932 on, he was exempt from military service during World War II. During this time he lived in Hampstead, and then in a flat in the Banbury Road in Oxford.

A close examination of his pictures shows sticks, stones, shells, leaves, and bits of fungi, all of which he would collect and bring home to his studio to study more closely. His largest picture is "The Battle of Britain", which measure 48 by 72 inches.

Henry Moore became an official war artist almost by mistake. Born in 1898, he was established as a sculptor by the time of the outbreak of war. As his materials became scarce, he turned inevitably to drawing and painting. After the fall of France, he applied to be trained as a munitions toolmaker, and waited at his home in Hampstead to be called; meanwhile the Germans had begun the bombing of London.

One evening he went home from the West End by Underground, where he saw thousands of people bedding down for the night; immeasurably moved by this, he made a number of sketches at home, and continued to go out at night, memorising the scenes and then drawing them at home. One of these "sketchbooks" he showed to Sir Kenneth Clark, who was on the Artists' Advisory Committee, and as a result Moore was asked to do a series of large drawings based on his sketches. In 1941 he did more than a hundred of these "shelter" drawings.

When the shelter drawings were finished, he looked around for another subject connected with the war–Herbert Read suggested he did a series of drawings of coal miners working at the pit face for the war effort. The War Artists' Advisory Committee sent him to Castleford, his birthplace, in January 1942; he stayed for two weeks, going down the mines every day to record the men at work. But the series of drawings which resulted from this lack the spontaneity and depth of feeling which are so obvious in his earlier war work.

Edward Ardizzone was appointed an Official War Office Artist in 1940. In that year he travelled through France and Belgium, returning through Boulogne. Until 1942 he worked in London, recording the Blitz, and in the west country and Northern Ireland. He then went to the Western Desert via South Africa, then to Sicily and Italy in 1943 to 1944, then to Normandy and Germany. His journeys are typical of many artists working under the scheme.

He kept a diary while he travel-

led around during the war, which gives a deeper understanding of his war drawings.

Probably the most famous of modern English painters, Graham Sutherland, born in 1903, began his working career as an engraver and etcher, turning to painting, at first mostly landscapes, in 1935. He was employed as an Official War Painter in World War II.

His drawings and paintings are of the devastation of streets and buildings gutted by fire, and of mines and furnaces worked by faceless creatures lit by oxyacetylene flares – whatever the subject it is lit by fires.

John Piper, born in 1903, is famous for his paintings of bomb damage in London and 18th Century Bath. His use of straight lines and angles show a gothic influence – as can be clearly seen in his study of air-raid shelters on page 3089. His pictures of ruined and bombed country houses are also famous, and his "Bristol South West Regional Headquarters" shows his gift for painting people.

Eric Ravilious, born in 1903, was one of the few official war

△ *Leslie Cole's oil painting "The Battle of the Sittang Bend". This work depicts vividly the adverse conditions with which the men of the 12th Army – in this case the Queen's Own (Royal West Kent) Regiment – often had to contend.*

◁ *Section of a watercolour of the Tokyo trials by Julius B. Stafford-Baker. He has included, in the foreground, his own sketching-board.*

△◁ *In realistic style, a U.S. Army painting of a tank destroyer in action.*

◁◁ *"The Black Watch Landing in Sicily at Red Beach" – a watercolour painted by Lieutenant Ian Eadie of the Gordon Highlanders.*

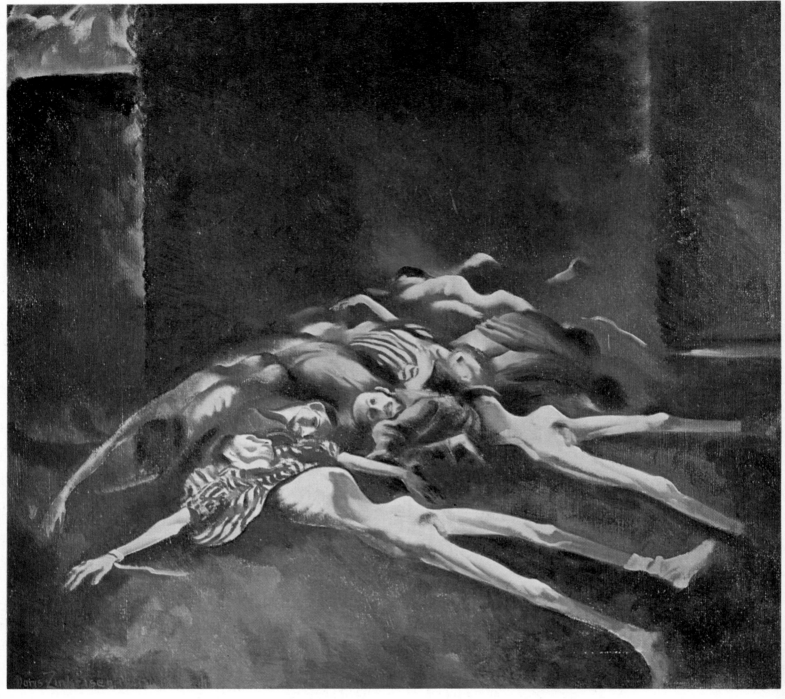

△ "Belsen"–an expressive and moving oil painting by Doris Zinkeisen which amply conveys the full horror of the concentration camps.

artists to die on active service during the war. As a student at the Royal College of Art he was taught by Paul Nash. Water-colour was his preferred medium, but he also did a number of woodcuts for book illustrations and decoration.

He joined the Royal Oberver Corps in 1939; in 1940 he was made a Captain in the Royal Marines and officially appointed as a war artist. In September 1942 he was flying from Iceland in a Coastal Command plane which disappeared, and by the next spring he was presumed killed in action. Many of his paintings are hung in the Imperial War Museum.

Stanley Spencer received no formal artistic training, but was later accepted at the Slade school where he won a scholarship. During World War I he was commissioned to do war paintings of the campaign in Macedonia, where he had served.

Although he did not serve actively in World War II, the War Artists' Advisory Committee commissioned him to do scenes of war work; in 1940 he went to Port Glasgow, to paint the shipyards. He was primarily a religious artist, and the cemetery at Port Glasgow had such an effect on him that he started another series of Resurrection paintings, two of which he completed in 1945 when

he returned to Cookham in Berkshire, whose churchyard had served as his original inspiration for Resurrection scenes.

Photographers at war

by Lionel Birch

To do justice to the work of a really comprehensive selection of World War II photographers would require tens of thousands of words. To assemble a really representative collection of World War II photographs would call for hundreds of pages. So many men from so many different Services, news agencies, newspapers, and magazines contributed in so many different theatres of war to the global pool of Allied war photographs that it is now often no longer possible to identify the individual photographer who took a particular striking picture. The credits may correctly say "U.S. Navy photograph" or "Ministry of Information photograph" or "Acme", or "Daily Mirror": but who exactly was the man who actually pressed the button of the camera at the decisive instant? Some of the most memorable pictures of the war were taken by that ubiquitous unknown soldier-cameraman

△ War-time photographers at work—press and film cameramen aboard a British convoy vessel during the early part of the war.
◁ The men who wrote the dispatches—war correspondents in the Burma jungle.

called Anonymous.

So there were scores of good World War II photographers for whom there is simply no room in these comparatively few pages. There were also a dozen or so really outstanding ones who are not represented here. But, among some of the outstanding photographers whose work does appear here, there is one man who was probably the greatest photographer, not only of World War II, but of the essence of War itself – Robert Capa. It was he who not only took the first classic picture of the instant of death-in-action during the Spanish Civil War, but also brought back the most vivid set of pictures from the first wave of the D-Day Normandy landings.

Capa, an ardent lover of life

and peace, who detested war and all the anguish which it inflicts on humanity, died at the age of 41. And for a large part of almost half that number of years he had been riding towards the sound of the guns. It was, in fact, Capa's irrepressible Say-Yes-to-Life attitude that finally carried him to his death, when in 1954 he was killed by a land mine in North Vietnam – in the fifth war, no less, that he had photographed.

War photographers come in all shapes and sizes, and with very varied human characteristics. To strangers who watched Capa dining and wining some of his countless friends and disciples with outrageous generosity in some of the more sophisticated restaurants of Paris, or doing crazy things on the ski-slopes of

Klosters, he would seem like no one's idea of a war photographer. He just did not look serious enough. Not, as the French say, "*sérieux*". To strangers interested in photography as a hobby, who observed the apparently feckless way in which he handled his camera and equipment, he looked like no one's idea of any kind of professional photographer at all. No; simply not serious enough.

Yet Capa, whose early life in Admiral Horthy's Hungary had been neither affluent nor easy, was a profoundly serious human being: far more serious than any politician in his concern for the human condition. He was as serious as he was gay – in the old sense of that now transmuted word: nobody loved women more fondly than he. And he took

▽ *A French* poilu *and a British "tommy" dive for cover from a machine-gunning German plane. With burning equipment forming the background, Marshall Perham's photo captures the grim days in France, 1940.*

both the seriousness and the gaiety with him in his heart and in the lens of his camera when he kissed the girls goodbye, and went off to his wars. The photographic record of his progress through various theatres of World War II underlines these two qualities, plus a third outstanding quality of his – compassion.

When Capa was photographing the London Blitz he detected in the people of Lambeth, and recorded with his camera, something akin to his own blend of seriousness and gaiety, which they used as a kind of Cockney secret weapon against the bombings and the devastation.

Capa's own recollections of his first tentative entry on to the scene of the North African campaign used to make hilarious

△ *The urgency of forward momentum is the same in any army. In this case, German infantrymen advance past an American half-track during the Ardennes offensive.*
◁ *Silhouetted against the sky, a U.S. Ranger scrambles along a rope during training at the Commando Depot in Scotland, February, 1943.*

post-war listening: how he had to get the famous American war correspondent, Ernie Pyle, and Bill Lang of *Time* magazine, to put him on the right road to the nearest bit of war. They directed him over the hills towards El Guetar. "Just ask anybody where the war is. You can't miss it," they said. Right they were. And, from that time on, Capa hardly ever ran short of a piece of war to photograph.

From North Africa to Sicily where, at Palermo, Capa and other war correspondents came up against what seemed to them to be quite unreasonable restrictions on their sphere of activity. H.Q.'s orders were that no war correspondents or Allied troops should enter the city, until the American commanding general arrived. This was on the grounds that the Italians there had stopped fighting, and the general wanted to receive their surrender in person (and perhaps be photographed doing it). These orders were energetically implemented by the military police. Of course, Capa got some pictures in Palermo later; but an

hour is a long time in a city that is in the process of surrendering, and the fleeting-opportunity first pictures of the face of defeat (or liberation?) that are missed, may never present themselves again.

From Sicily, Capa went on with the invading forces to Italy; and the the melancholy of Naples, where children who for a fortnight had fought the Germans with stolen weapons were being buried, after being killed by their German elders and, in the end, betters.

And so to Britain, in the days of preparation for the opening of the Second Front.

To go, or not to go, with the first wave of American troops on D-Day: that was the question – and the agony of having a war correspondent's privileged free choice – which confronted him. Capa, who was never one to resist a gamble, opted to go. His own account of his D-Day experiences, published in his book *Images of War,* make one of the most evocative pieces of verbal reporting of the war. His photographic *reportage* of D-Day was

the victim of a melancholy accident in the London darkroom where his films were being processed. The emulsion ran; and, of the 106 pictures he took of the landings on the "Easy Red" beach of Normandy, only eight saw the light of day. In the event, his eight surviving pictures were more than enough to "tell it as it was."

From Normandy, Capa followed through with the advancing Allies, and dropped by parachute with the airborne troops on the far side of the Rhine. From there, he went on all the way to the bitter end, until the moment when he took the haunting picture of one of the last soldiers to die in the war in Europe.

Robert Capa, a Hungarian who became a naturalised citizen of the United States, operated mostly during World War II alongside American forces. George Rodger, who is British, operated with an astonishing variety of troops – American, British, Free French, Indian, Free Poles, Sudan Defence Force, Free Yugoslavs, Gurkhas – in 63 different countries right across the warring world, in a maverick style that

◁ *Tense and alert, a G.I. charges forward through a hail of Japanese machine gun bullets on Okinawa, May 1945.*

Colour photography really "came of age" during World War II. In particular, German and American photographers made full use of facilities available to them to take the very best shots possible.

△ Cold and bored, an American infantryman stands on guard with the stark landscape of Iceland as a backdrop.

◁ Streams of tracer bullets show up against the dark sky as a rear-gunner on a night flight tests his guns. This photograph, in the idiom of the era, is dramatically called "The Road to Berlin".

▷ British craftsmanship at its best – 83-year-old swordsmith Tom Beasley forges the blade of the Stalingrad Sword. This Sword of Honour was presented to the people of Stalingrad in recognition of their heroic defence of the city.

was unique.

In 1939, Rodger was working in London as a freelance photographer, after doing a two-year stretch with B.B.C. Television at Alexandra Palace, when *Life* magazine commissioned him to do a photographic essay on wartime London. After that, the magazine took him on as a full-time stringer, and he started by covering various phases of the Battle of Britain, the Dunkirk evacuation, the London Blitz – picture stories which were also sold to *Picture Post* and *Illustrated*.

His first foreign assignment was a stint with Colonel (later General) Leclerc in West Africa, where he was temporarily accredited to General de Gaulle's Free French. This six-week assignment ended for Rodger two years later, in Calcutta, after he had escaped from the Japanese in Burma. He made his way home via India, the Middle East, Sudan, Chad, Liberia, Brazil, Trinidad, Miami, New York, and Greenland – a ready-made, but unaccredited, war photographer. The record of that marathon trip is contained in two books of George Rodger's, *Desert Journey* and *Red Moon Rising,* which were published in the United States in one volume called *Far on the Ringing Plains.*

The number of campaigns covered by Rodger in the course of the war is breath-taking. They include: the takeover of the Cameroons and Gabon by de Gaulle from the Vichy French; Colonel Leclerc's epic march into Libya and his capture of Kufra Oasis; the Eritrean Campaign, with the Sudan Defence Force; the Ethiopian campaign with the 4th Indian Division; the war in the Western Desert, accredited to the Free French; the Rashid Ali rebellion, Iraq, with the R.A.F.; the Syrian campaign against the Vichy French, with General Catroux of France Libre; the first Burma campaign, and the retreat,

accredited to General Stilwell; the North African landing, with General Mark Clark's U.S. Forces; Monte Cassino, with the Gurkhas; the D-Day Normandy landings at Arromanches, with the British; the liberation of Paris; and of Brussels; the Walcheren campaign and the liberation of Holland; the relief of Belsen; the German Lüneberg surrender to Montgomery; and the liberation of Copenhagen.

Throughout, Rodger was very much a loner. He preferred to operate independently, with his own transport. (He was given a very adequate expense account by *Life* magazine.) Rodger feels that,

Press photographers were always on the look-out for the unusual or odd to catch for the entertainment of the public.

△ *The Anderson shelter as part of the family – complete with rock garden, goldfish on the roof, and carpet at the entrance.*

△▷ *Curiously cheerful under the circumstances, two German nuns steer a cart of supplies through the snowy streets of Aachen.*

▷ *The sort of photograph beloved by newspaper editors during the war – amusing, defiant, and sentimental at the same time.*

as he had a roving commission over a vast area – Morocco to Burma – and no orthodox official recognition as a war photographer, that was probably the best way. "I was attached to so many odd armies," he explains, "that finally I had a composite uniform made up, which seemed to be acceptable almost anywhere."

He says that he had no "favourite" war subjects: he found them all very upsetting. "I worked very much on feature material among the people of

different races who were themselves involuntarily involved when their homelands became battlefields. In this way I could emphasise the horror, the wastefulness and the pure folly of war – and this I preferred. I covered the campaigns, the concentration camps, the landings, and the battles, not because I liked it, but because they had to be shown. In fact, I found that combat pictures of the Don McCullin type were hard to come by in the Second World War (particularly as I had no orthodox papers), on account

of the lack of facilities and a really keyed-up Public Relations organisation."

Rodger believes that, up until D-Day, he was probably the only British still photographer who was not operating under military orders in the Army Film and Photographic Unit, where, in the view of the War Office, all photographers belonged. "In spite of the fact that I was employed by *Life* magazine – who published some of my photographs almost every week – and I was therefore in a unique position to further

British propaganda in America where we needed all the support we could get, Whitehall considered my position most irregular, and tried to insist that I should return home to be enrolled as a sergeant in the Army Film and Photographic Unit.

"But P.R.O.s in the field had a very different attitude, and restricted me only when they were under duress to do so. I remember one P.R.O. coming to see me and saying to me, over an evening drink, 'Look, old boy, you'd better disappear from here in the night,

because I have orders to come and arrest you tomorrow morning.' Even when the top P.R. Officer in Cairo, Brigadier Sir Philip Astley, was obliged to tear my pseudo badges off my shoulders, he did it with obvious reluctance. In general, I found P.R.O.'s very willing, and very helpful within the rather restricted limits of the facilities they were allowed to offer.

"Anyhow, by dodging from army to army I managed to hold out; and finally I got myself properly accredited to the British Forces in time for the D-Day landings in Normandy."

There were extremely few British "still" war photographers who, like George Rodger, eventually achieved the status of War Correspondent. The majority of war photographers were members

△ ◁ *The gaunt ruins of Cassino, looking more like a film set than a real town.*
◁ *"Somewhere in Italy"—the weight of American industry makes itself felt. Thousands of vehicles are gathered for the "Dragoon" landings in southern France.*
△ *New weapons, new techniques, make interesting photographs: a Spitfire about to tip over a V-1.*

3119

◁ A Union Jack flies defiantly over the rubble of Coventry after an air raid in November 1940. Although the heart of the city, including the cathedral, was almost totally destroyed, the morale of the people was not broken.

△ In one of the most famous photographs of the war, the dome of St. Paul's rises intact above the smoke of burning London – a sight which epitomised to the capital's residents, and the whole country, the will to survive and eventually to win.

▷ Sunset over Auschwitz. This Russian photograph shows the strangely peaceful – even beautiful – remains of the death camp where more than two million people were killed.

American war photographer Robert Capa followed the G.I.s and recorded their experiences in battle and on the march.
▽ In the rubble-strewn streets of the town, an Italian officer gives the Americans a welcome drink.
▷ On one of the last days of the war in Europe–May 5, 1945– Capa was with the troops in Leipzig. Sheltering in a building, he took a remarkable series of photographs of an American machine-gunner setting up his post and then being killed by a sniper's bullet.

of the Army Film and Photographic Unit, working strictly under British Army orders. Besides these two categories, there were also, during the early days of the war, a few civilian home-based independent photographers. One such was John Topham, a Kent-based freelance who made an international reputation with his photographs of the Battle of Britain, and particularly with his picture of hop-pickers' children sheltering from German bombers in a slit trench in Kent.

Topham, who was born in 1908, had started his working life as a policeman in the East End of London, where he was not averse to taking pictures on the beat– an unusual and distinctly irregular proceeding. Some of these pictures he sold to national newspapers; and in 1933 he gave up what he considered a boring life as a policeman, and set up as a freelance photographer. Since then he has never worked for anyone but himself (apart from four years working for King and Country as a war-time R.A.F. station Intelligence Officer). By the time war broke out, Topham was an established freelance operating from Sidcup in Kent, at

the centre of the district where most of the early action in the air occurred. "It was," he says, "a matter of going–or trying to go– where the trouble was. The national newspapers would ring up and say 'We hear there's terrible damage at such-and-such a place. We can't get there: can you?' "

It was not easy, with all the restrictions on movement then prevailing in anticipation of a German airborne and seaborne invasion. "I had a Ministry of Information pass, but as often as not the Home Guard wouldn't let you through. So I had to go round

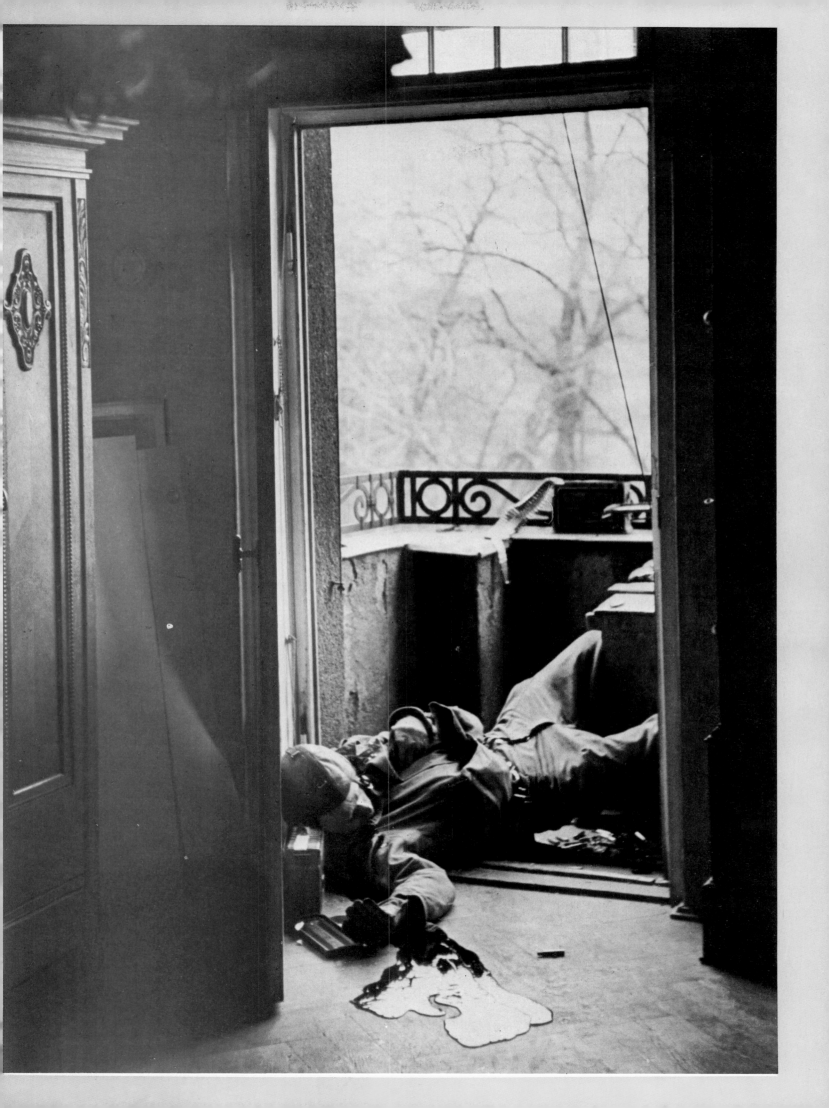

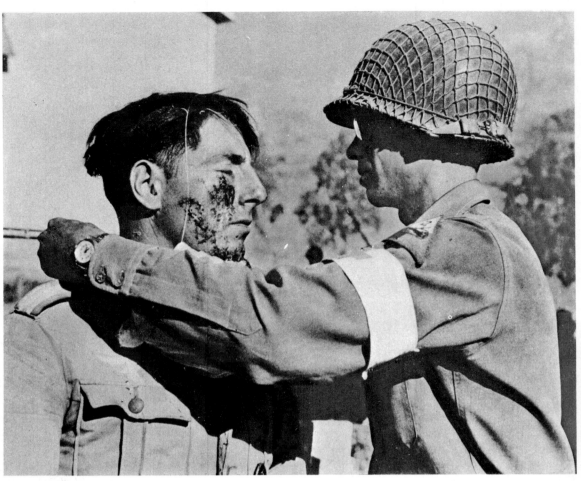

fire-fighting forces at the height of the Blitz. Every night for two weeks he slept at a fire station; but, oddly, the bombers were giving London a respite. And then, in one single night when the capital was turned into a blazing inferno of flame and smoke, Hardy took a series of epic pictures which really opened the eyes of people throughout Britain and farther afield as to what it was really like to be a London fire-fighter. From September 1938, when *Picture Post* was launched, until February 1, 1941 when this feature of Hardy's appeared, no photographer had ever had his name attached in print to any set of pictures published in the magazine. But now Hopkinson, evidently feeling that Hardy had brought off something of an

by the back to get there," Topham explains. "Also, it was sometimes possible to hoodwink people. I had a black M.G. similar to the kind the Kent police were using at that time. And on one occasion a reporter friend and I managed to get shepherded along in the very front of a procession in which King George was doing an inspection tour. We had no passes; but, by the end, I did have some nice pictures." During this time Topham had a contract with *Life* magazine, who paid him extra for anything they published.

He photographed aerial dog-fights and vapour trail patterns, crashes of German and British planes, bomb damage, people being rescued from the debris; and he took some vivid pictures of a blazing oil refinery at Thameshaven, which were quashed by the censor. Once, he landed up with a coastal battery at Shorne, near Gravesend, where the gunners were getting up a can-can show of their own; and he photographed them as they rushed off to man the guns in their frilly dresses. Another time, he made a picture feature of a show given by the girls from the Windmill ("We never closed") Theatre. "I got back home at five in the morning," he recalls jovially,

"and my wife accused me of having raped the lot of them!"

The period of the Battle of Britain was a time of inevitable suspicious alertness. "I used to have the cops calling at my place at least once a week," says Topham. "People had reported that they'd seen me taking pictures. After I had photographed some chaps digging slit trenches at Blackheath, for instance, two C.I.D. men called on me and absolutely refused to recognise my Ministry of Information pass." After a lot of argument, Topham decided to destroy the plates. "Men digging trenches didn't make all that interesting pictures anyway."

In 1941 Topham joined the R.A.F. as a photographer, but was soon diverted into Intelligence. After the war, both the *New Chronicle* and the *Evening News* asked him to come on their staffs, but he declined: he even refused any retainer. "I never wanted to be tied up or tied down."

A rare and very independent kind of man, John Topham. Inevitably less independent was the main body of British war photographers who were enrolled in the Army Film and Photographic Unit: a military outfit which had one of the highest

casualty rates per size of unit in the whole of the British Army. In most theatres of the war the unit was composed of men with the rank of captain or sergeant, with a major as Officer Commanding. Alan Whicker, for instance, was a captain in the A.F.P.U. So was the late Edward G. Malindine, who had taken pictures during the Spanish Civil War and then, after a spell as a freelance, had joined the photographic staff of the *Daily Herald*, and of *Illustrated* magazine. His memorable picture of an incident in the war that came to Norway is on page 3210.

Another member of the A.F.P.U.—one who later became world-famous as a combat war photographer through his sequences of photographs of the Inchon landings and other actions of the Korean War—was Bert Hardy. He carried the rank of sergeant throughout his time in the European theatre until, after V.E. Day, he went out to the Far East and was made a Captain.

Hardy had been asked in 1940 by Tom Hopkinson, editor of *Picture Post,* to join the magazine's staff as a photographer. One of his first major assignments was to make a picture feature on the work of London's unprecedented kind, decided to break with precedent. "From our rule of anonymity we except these pictures," he wrote. "They were taken by A. Hardy, one of our own cameramen."

Many of the other Blitz stories photographed by Hardy in 1940–41 were done in the East End, where Hardy, who is a pungent and fruity example of the eternal Cockney, was in his element. "The East End at War", the "Life of an East End Person", "Morning after the Blitz" were some of them. And there was one characteristic single picture of a man sitting among the debris of his bombed home, and solemnly and conscientiously filling in his Income Tax Return form. Hardy also went along with the Navy who were hunting E-boats in the North Sea, and with the Marines who were staging a mock invasion landing from the sea—in rowing boats!

In June 1942, Hardy went into the Army, and eventually was sent on a six-week photographic course, where he had to work with a Super Ikonta camera "with a silly tripod"—and with an instructor who reckoned that 35-millimetre cameras were ridiculous. Still, he came out top of the course, and was then attached, with the two men who came second and third, to Public Relations in London. It was a toss-up which of the three photographers should go on the Dieppe raid, and the one that did go lost his life there.

In Normandy Hardy, now a sergeant in the Army Film and Photographic Unit, was able to think up a lot of his own story ideas. His aim was to try and do one picture feature a week for *Picture Post* and *Illustrated*: stories such as what actually happens to a man who is badly wounded in the front line; and features in Paris, Antwerp, and Brussels. There were also pictures which suddenly presented themselves—as when, on the west bank of the Rhine, General Dempsey suddenly whistled up Hardy and his camera, to take a picture of him crossing the river. That, Bert feels, was really intended as one for the history books.

Hardy was conscious of a certain amount of frustration and restriction, simply as a result of his having the rank of sergeant. "Unlike the War Correspondents,

◁ An American medical corpsman gives first aid to an enemy soldier captured at Palermo as U.S. troops over-ran the town during the conquest of Sicily: another of Capa's superb studies of people.
▽ A poignant reminder of the hatreds and injustices unleashed by war. A mother, "found guilty" of collaboration, has had her head forcibly shaved. Capa's photograph captures the glee—and malice—on the faces of her neighbours.

you couldn't use the Officers' Mess, for instance: and that meant you could miss hearing about a lot of things happening that might have made good pictures."

Later, Hardy went out as a captain to the Far East, where he seems to have had all the facilities he could have wished for. From his photographic output there you might think—not quite accurately—that he had become Lord Mountbatten's personal photographer.

Another member of the A.F.P.U., who later made a name for himself, first as a still photographer on *Picture Post,* and subsequently as a cameraman with B.B.C. Television, was Slim Hewitt.

Hewitt became a war photographer in a distinctly unorthodox way. Before the war he had taken a few pictures for his own pleasure, some of which he had sold. At the end of 1940, he enlisted in the Royal Engineers as a driver; and drove in Egypt, Syria, and the Sinai desert. From El Alamein onwards to Sicily and Italy, he served as a batman-driver. One day, on the road to Cassino, Hewitt's officer, who had seen some photographs that

◁ *A Russian mother searches for her 18-year-old son outside Kerch'.*
▽ ◁ ◁ *J. W. Malindine's photograph of a Norwegian civilian and his small daughter fleeing to the beach at Vaagsö. They were later evacuated to England by British commandos.*

Two photographs smuggled out of Poland in 1940 by a British photographer.
▽ ◁ *A young boy rescues his pet canary from the ruins of his Warsaw home.*
▽ *This girl has found the body of her elder sister, just killed in a field by a strafing aircraft.*

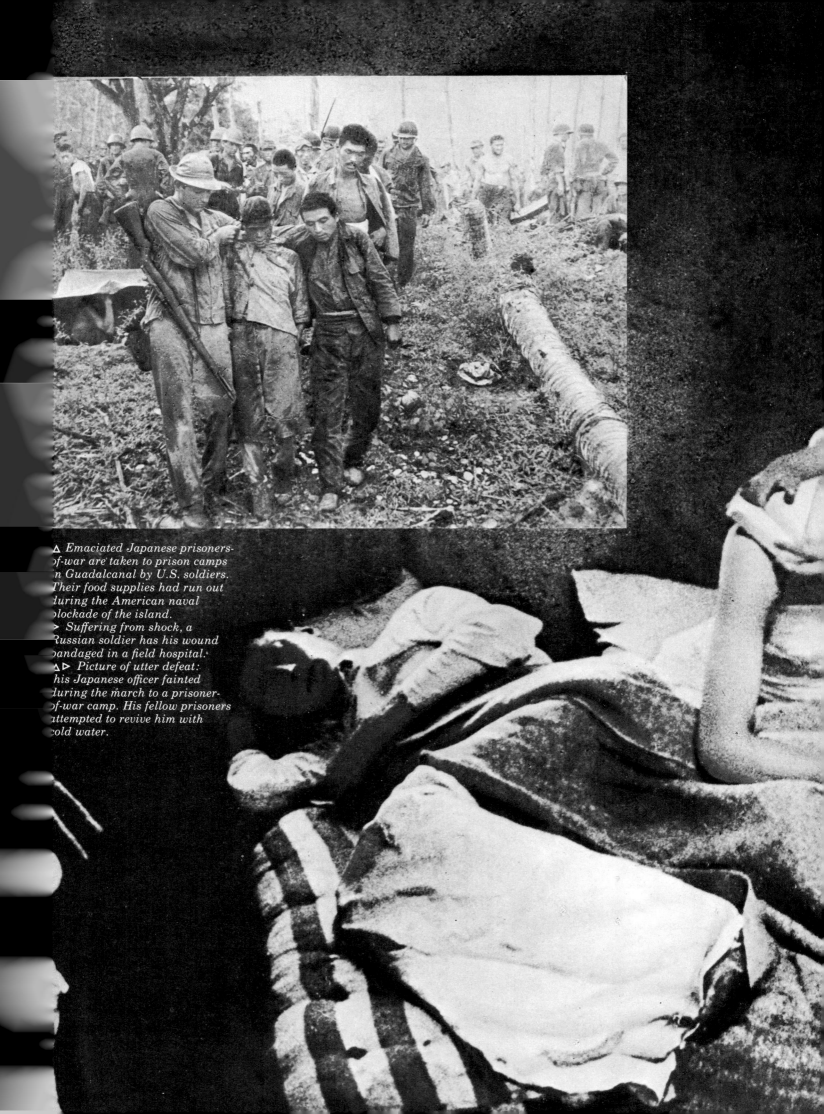

△ Emaciated Japanese prisoners-
of-war are taken to prison camps
n Guadalcanal by U.S. soldiers.
Their food supplies had run out
during the American naval
blockade of the island.
▷ Suffering from shock, a
Russian soldier has his wound
bandaged in a field hospital.
△ ▷ Picture of utter defeat:
his Japanese officer fainted
during the march to a prisoner-
of-war camp. His fellow prisoners
attempted to revive him with
cold water.

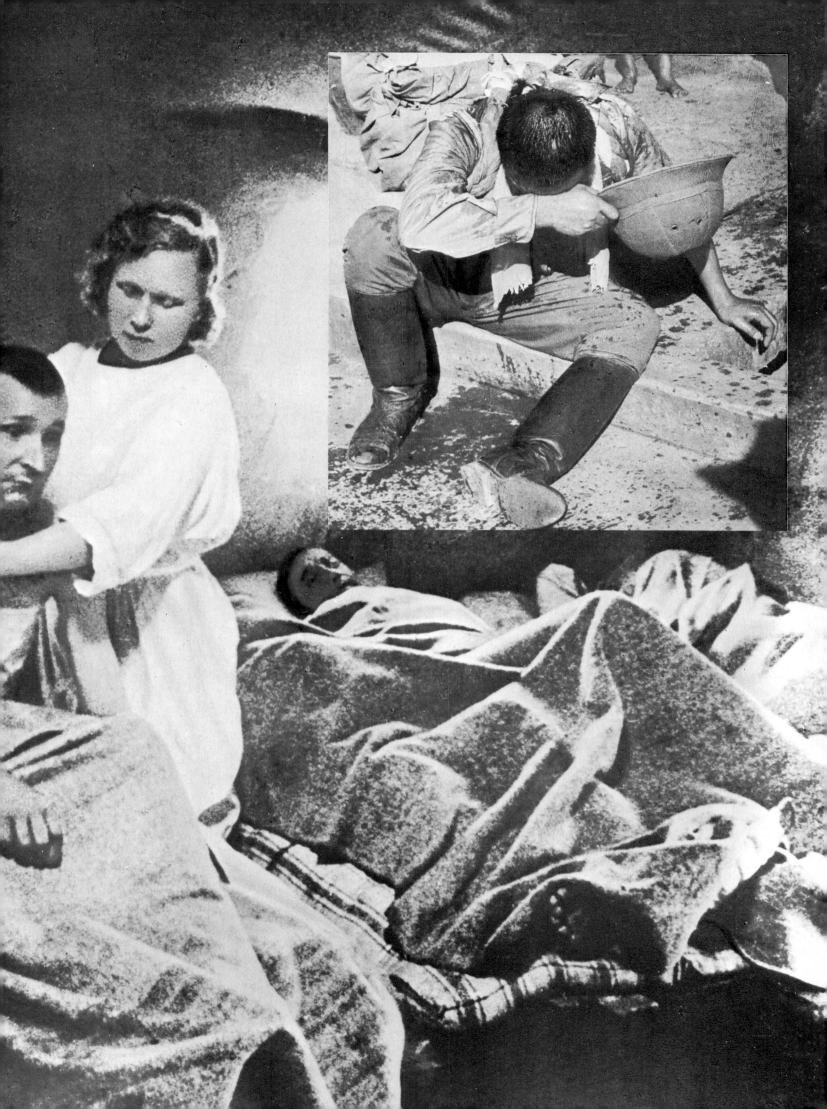

Slim had taken with his own camera, suddenly, as their vehicle was passing an A.F.P.U. tent by the roadside, shouted "Stop". The officer went into the tent, and later summoned Hewitt, who found himself in the presence of an A.F.P.U. captain. The captain said "I don't know anything about you, but this officer has given you the hell of a recommendation."

Thereupon, Hewitt became a member of the unit and, from being an unpaid acting lance-corporal, was made up to sergeant –but without a sergeant's pay, because he had never taken a trade course. For that course he had to go back to Britain, and Pinewood Studios, where one of the instructors told him: "I want you to be able to take pictures like the six I'm just going to show you." Four out of those six photographs turned out to be ones which Hewitt had taken himself in Italy. They were, he explains, "reconstructed" pictures (and explicity stated to be such) of the New Zealanders in action at Cassino.

After the Pinewood course, Hewitt was made up to sergeant, officially and with pay this time. He arrived in Normandy on D+5 where the transit camp authorities said they had never heard of the A.F.P.U.; and anyway, they pointed out, there was a great shortage of drivers. After that was sorted out, Hewitt went on with his military photographic unit up to Brussels, the Ardennes, Belsen, and Berlin.

The restrictions of which he was most conscious concerned his regulation equipment. "I was obliged to cover an important crossing of the Rhine with a Voigtlander-Besser issue camera, which would probably have retailed before the war at about £6," he says. "Later I did get issued with a Rolleiflex. But we had no miniature cameras or telephoto lenses–which put us of the A.F.P.U. at a disadvantage with the War Correspondents, who could bring over whatever equipment they pleased. For us, the trouble was that the Ministry of Information insisted on a large square negative . . . That ruled out all 35-millimetres stuff."

Hewitt says that he was required to spend a lot of his time doing propaganda and morale-boosting pictures: for instance, "British soldier inside Germany for the first time befriends lost dog whimpering in the ruins". And, one November, he recalls,

"we photographed soldiers pretending to make Christmas puddings out of mud, with petrol sprinkled over the mud, for the morale of the people back home." There were occasional instructions such as: "Don't take any more pictures of soldiers wearing glasses."

Hewitt feels that his best picture of the war was undoubtedly one that he took at the liberation of Belsen. "There was this pathetic skeleton of an old woman standing naked in the hut, with a snapshot of herself when young just beside her. And she was shrieking at me: 'Take a picture of me! I want the whole world to see what they have done to me.' She died next day. I reckon" Hewitt concludes, "that one solitary figure can be more eloquent than a whole heap of bodies."

A very rare breed of British war photographers was those who had the status of War Correspondents, such as Jack Esten, the late Cecil Warhurst of *The Times* newspapers, and the late Jimmy Crayford. These men, who wore army uniform with War Correspondent shoulder flashes but no pips, did not come under the military command of the Army Film and Photographic Unit. They were responsible to the Newspaper Proprietors' Association.

Jack Esten was working for the *Daily Herald* and the magazine *Illustrated* when he was asked, some time before D-Day, to volunteer as a War Correspondent photographer. But he and Warhurst and Crayford were disappointed to find that, when D-Day came, they were still in London. "The Army Film and Photographic Unit seemed to think they could cope," Esten recalls. "Yet practically all the first pictures of the Normandy landings that were published seemed to be American.

"So," Esten relates, "I decided to hitch-hike myself unofficially

Field-Marshal Rommel was not only an imaginative military leader, but an expert cameraman as well. These photographs demonstrate his skill.
△ ◁ *Rommel's tanks reach the northern coast of France in an attempt to cut off British and French troops in 1940.*
△ *German transports in the Libyan desert, viewed from Rommel's Storch aircraft.*
◁ *German troops pass carts abandoned by refugees.*

Three more photographs taken by
Field-Marshal Rommel.
▽ St. Valéry, where Rommel
captured General Fortune of the
51st (Highland) Division during
the invasion of France in 1940.
▷ Rommel kept both Axis troops
and Arabs happy in North Africa
by organising "desert Derbies".
▷▷ French P.O.W.s under the
watchful eyes of their captors
during the fall of France.

across to France. I had an Army uniform and a naval pass which was to enable me just to visit a ship that was loading. But I found an American naval captain who was going to the British beaches in Normandy; and, when I got across, I went on to Bayeux and stayed there, with a suitcase, for five days. I brought back home a lot of pictures – of the wounded and P.O.W.s – which were completely unofficial; but they did get published."

Then Esten, in company with Warhurst and Crayford, were sent to wait three days on Hackney Marshes, where the V-1 "buzz-bombs" were dropping, for transport to take them to the British floating harbour at Arromanches. Thence, later, though they had no conducting officers at that time, they made their way to General Montgomery's headquarters, where some of the first Russian Staff Officers seen on the Western Front were paying a visit. Esten asked to be allowed to photograph the Russians with Montgomery. He was told he could photograph the Russians – but not with General Montgomery. Apparently photographing Montgomery was the prerogative of the Army Film and Photographic Unit. "I only photographed Monty once all the way to Brussels – when I caught him on the hop, by luck, handing cigarettes around to the troops."

Esten's determined refusal to photograph the Russians, without Monty being in the picture, made him *persona non grata* with the military authorities. However he was allowed to press on for a while with the advancing Allies; and he and a cine-photographer colleague actually managed to get in to the town of Rouen ahead of the Canadian troops.

Later, when he came back to Britain for a bit of leave, he found .that he was not going to be allowed to go back to continental Europe, "because I had complained about the Army Film Unit isolating us few War Correspondent Photographers."

After Victory in Europe Day, Esten started out on a facility trip with the R.A.F. which was by now engaged in reinforcing the

These photographs of Hitler in action were taken by the Führer's personal cameraman, Heinrich Hoffman.
Inset: *Captured film showing the last photographs of Hitler, taken on his 56th birthday. He committed suicide ten days later.*

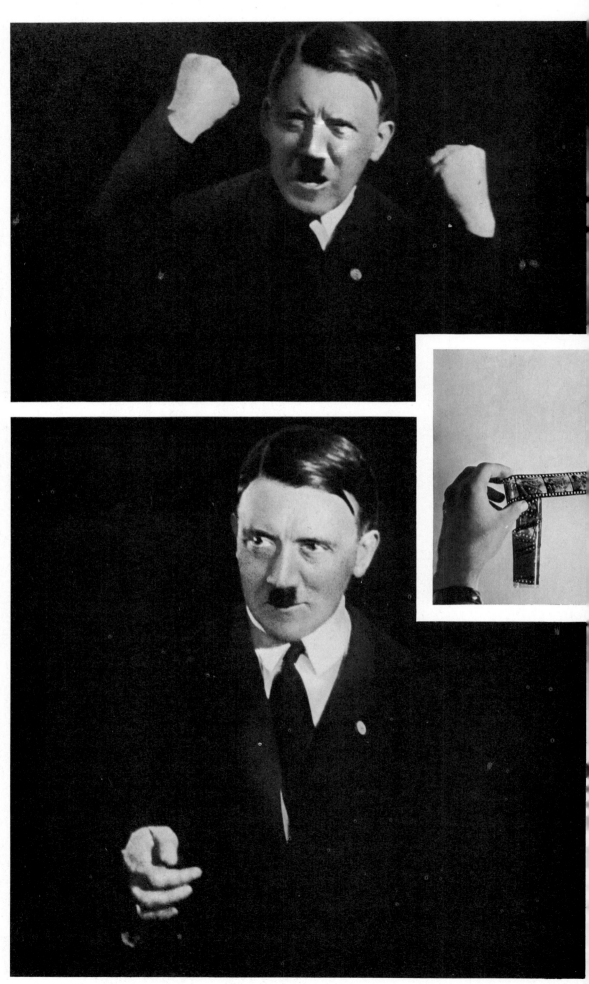

Far East forces by air. Finding himself stuck in Karachi, he hitch-hiked across India to Rangoon, and got himself accredited to South-East Asia Command, in time to photograph the liberation of Singapore. There he took a set of pictures of a Japanese general surrendering, which included one photograph of a British officer kicking the Japanese general on the head. That particular picture Esten was instructed to suppress. A photograph of his, showing the general prostrating himself after being reprimanded, was passed and published. The picture of the kicking was killed, however.

And there is Henri Cartier-Bresson, a master photographer whom one does not think of primarily as a war photographer. He spent the first three-quarters of the war in a P.O.W. camp, but when he managed to escape, he started to use his miniature camera to make an unforgettable record of the European scene after Paris had been liberated and the tide of war had begun to recede.

▷ *English schoolchildren hide in a slit trench in the hopfields of Kent while above them a dog fight is in progress during the Battle of Britain. John Topham's photograph catches their expression of rapt interest.*
▽ *One of the happier moments in the Kutno ghetto.*

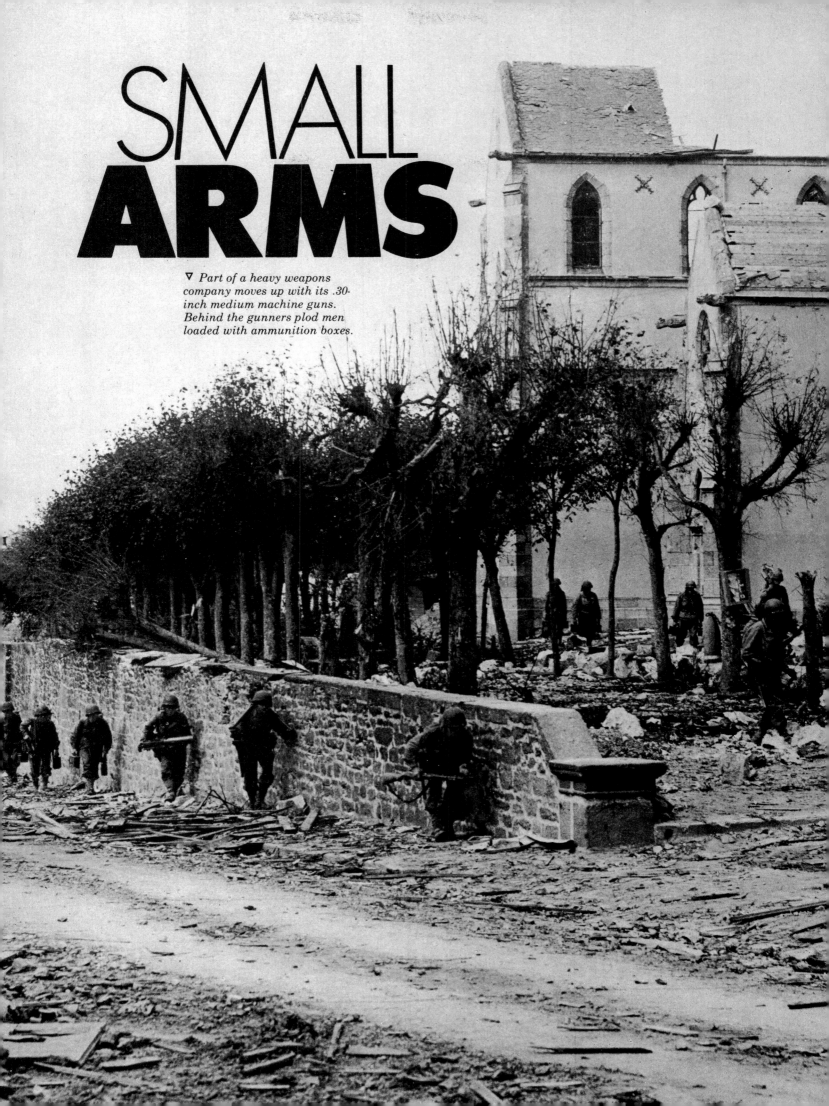

SMALL ARMS

▽ *Part of a heavy weapons company moves up with its .30-inch medium machine guns. Behind the gunners plod men loaded with ammunition boxes.*

THE M3 SUB-MACHINE GUN (U.S.A.)

In 1941, when the United States' entry into the war was inevitable in the foreseeable future, the armaments staff of the U.S. Army put in hand a programme of research and tests on possible sub-machine guns to be used along-side the Thompson. The weapons they evaluated were of American and foreign origin, and included the German MP38 and the Bergmann 34, although these had not, of course, been offered by their manufacturers.

Among the guns presented for selection was a product of the firm High Standard, which was very similar in line to the Thompson M21–a clear proof of the great influence that the old "Typewriter" had had on American tastes. 32.2 inches long (barrel 11 inches) this sub-machine gun has two grips and a stock, like the M21. It uses a box magazine holding 20 rounds, and weighs about 9.12 pounds. Its calibre is, however, not the usual .45-inch but the 9-mm Parabellum, a European calibre. Made by Marlin in rather limited quantities, it was distributed to the United Defense Supply Corporation under the designation U.D. M42.

Although the Thompson M1, adopted in April of 1942, had proved itself perfectly adequate in all conditions of war, it still had one drawback: it was expen-

▽ *Men of the Ammunition and Pioneer Platoon of an American infantry division prepare to enter a house in Brest. The soldier on the left has an M3A1 sub-machine gun, the one in the centre an M1 rifle, and the one on the right a Thompson M1.*

△ *The American M3 sub-machine gun. This was adopted in December 1942 as an eventual replacement for the Thompson M1, which was expensive to produce and not adequate for field service. The improved M3A1 was adopted in December 1944.*

▽ *The American Thompson M1928 A1 sub-machine gun. Early models all had a Cutts compensator (attached to the muzzle to stop the weapon "climbing" during automatic fire), radial cooling fins on the barrel, and leaf rear sights.*

▽▽ *The American Thompson M1 sub-machine gun. This was a simplified version of the M1928A1, with a fixed aperture rear sight and no cooling fins or compensator. Unlike the M1928A1, the M1 could take only the box magazine.*

△▷ *Members of an American patrol near Livergnano in Italy. From left to right, the weapons are the .3-inch M1903A4 sniper rifle (adopted in 1942), the .3-inch M1 rifle (adopted in 1936), and the .45-inch Thompson M1 sub-machine gun.*

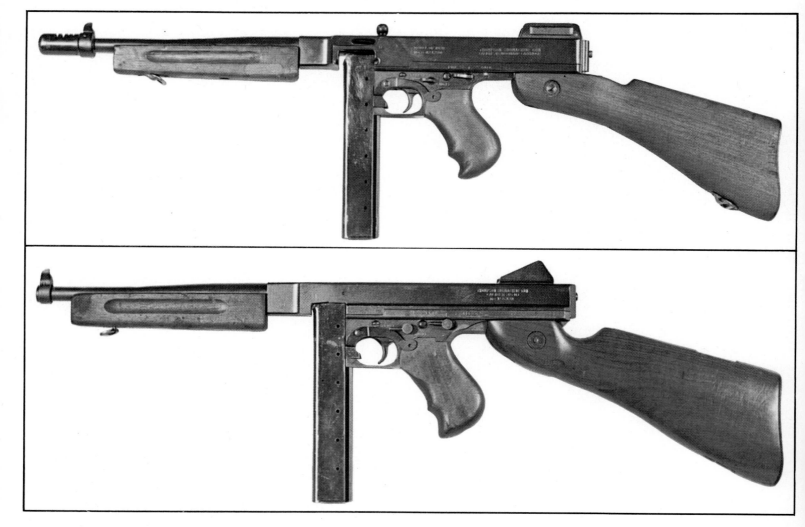

sive and needed skilled workmanship, using complex machine tools. The Americans tried, therefore, to design a cheaper and simpler weapon which would be even handier and lighter in weight. The result was the **M3 sub-machine gun,** issued from December 1942.

The M3 is robust and of simple technical and mechanical construction. It is short, with a grip and retractable stock, and is closer in design to a pistol than to a service rifle. It was inspired by the British Sten gun, and built in stamped steel plate, which was cheaper and made for quicker production, but was nevertheless extremely effective. The calibre was still the .45-inch of the cartridge of the Thompson M1. However, as it was obvious that America could supply her British allies as well as resistance forces, the M3 was also made in 9-mm Parabellum calibre, which was almost universally used in European sub-machine guns.

The M3 operates on the blowback principle and is capable of automatic fire only. It is essentially a close-combat weapon. It uses an in-line box magazine holding 30 rounds. It has an extendable stock composed of two steel rods. Its barrel is 8 inches long, overall length is 29.8 inches, and retracted length 22.8 inches. It weighs 8.15 pounds. A hinged plate covers the ejection port; this plate, when closed, acts as an extra safety device. There is also an external lever for cocking the weapon. In a later model, the M3A1 (1944), the gun was further simplified and strengthened. The

cocking lever was eliminated and the ejection port cover was enlarged. In both models, with a .45-inch cartridge, the muzzle velocity of the bullet is 920 feet per second. The cyclic rate is 350–450 rounds per minute.

THE THOMPSON M1928A1 & M1 SUB-MACHINE GUNS (U.S.A.)

There are some weapons that have the unenviable distinction of being representative of an age and mentality, and the Thompson sub-machine gun is such a one–a hero of the "Roaring Twenties".

Such fame probably never even crossed the mind of the soldier who gave his name to one of the most famous automatic weapons in the world. General J. T. Thompson, graduated from West Point Military Academy in 1882. In 1916, on the eve of America's entry into the war against Germany, Thompson, already a general, started work on his own automatic rifle, in .30-inch calibre, which was ready in 1917. This weapon was not successful, however, and never saw action.

In the last months of 1918, when knowledge of light automatic weapons using pistol-power ammunition had become general, Thompson set out on the same course as the Europeans Revelli and Schmeisser, and created, with the help of his son Marcellus and the engineer T. E. Eickhoff, a submachine gun which used the .45-inch pistol round. Production of this weapon was entrusted to the Warner & Swassey Company of Cleveland, and later, at the end of

1919 or the beginning of 1920, a company was founded in New York for the production and distribution of the Thompson. The weapon was called the M19, but it was not until the M21 appeared that the Thompson began to be famous.

It was the particular social conditions of America at this period that made the Thompson famous. Prohibition had generated a profitable black market in alcohol, organised by powerful rival gangster organisations. It was at this time that the Thompson got its colourful nicknames– the "Typewriter", the "Burpgun", the "Chopper", the "Tommy Gun", and so on–nicknames which reflected the lethal power and rate of fire possessed by the Thompson.

The M21 is delayed blowback-operated and has a fixed barrel and a recoiling breech-block. The breech-block remains fixed until the bullet has emerged from the barrel. The hesitation locking device is based on the friction of two sloping surfaces, and to ensure a regular functioning, the sliding surfaces are constantly lubricated by felt pads soaked in oil.

The weapon is 31.8 inches long; without its magazine it weighs 9.6 pounds; its rear sight is calibrated up to 750 yards. The detachable magazines are of three kinds: a drum with 100 rounds arranged in a spiral; a drum with 50 rounds; and a vertical box with 20 rounds. The drum magazine is rather heavy, and indeed with 100 rounds loaded the Thompson weighs as much as 18.7 pounds. Perhaps for this reason, and to make it easier to hold, it is fitted with two grips,

one behind the trigger and the other beneath the barrel. It is capable of automatic or semi-automatic fire, at the rate of 1,500 rounds per minute in the first case and 100 in the second.

Used by gangsters and, in much larger numbers, by the police, the Thompson M21 was not adopted by the United States Army. In 1928 there appeared a new model, which differed from the previous one on several points–for instance, the cyclic rate of fire was reduced to 600–700 rounds per minute. This model, the M1928, was adopted in 1932 by the U.S. Army in a modified form, the **M1928A1,** which has a single grip and a fixed rear sight instead of the calibrated one. It is a little heavier than the M21 (10.75 pounds) and a little longer (33.75 inches) because it has a compensator. The calibre is still .45-inch and the cartridge is that of the Colt automatic pistol. The box magazine holds 20 or 30 rounds.

With this assault weapon the United States entered World War II. It did, however, still have certain serious disadvantages, such as a high production cost and the unreliability of the hesitation breech lock, which was apt to jam. So the Auto Ordnance Corporation, which made the Thompson, produced two modified versions, the **M1** and the **M1A1,** which was one of the most common American sub-machine guns of the last war. The M1 and the M1A1 are 32 inches long (barrel 10.5 inches) and weigh 10.45 pounds. They use 20- or 30-round box magazines. The cyclic rate of fire is 700 rounds per minute.

3142

THE GARAND M1 RIFLE AND THE M1 CARBINE (U.S.A.)

The U.S. entered the war having already started to equip their infantry with a semi-automatic rifle: the Garand M1. Although by September 1941 only 60,000 Garands had been issued, everything was set for an enormous production: in the three and a half years in which the U.S.A. were at war over 4,040,000 rifles were supplied to the Army.

The story of the Garand M1 began in 1920, when John Garand, whose semi-automatic rifle had been tried but not approved by the Army, was taken on as a designer by the military arsenal of Springfield to work on a new weapon. In 1929 the fruit of his labours was tried out, together with other semi-automatic rifles, and was chosen as the best, although it was not perfect: this would be the prototype, and steps would be taken to improve it.

Garand's rifle was made and tested in two calibres, .30-inch and .276-inch. With the first the .30/06 cartridge was used, from the ordinary Springfield bolt-action rifle used by the American Army; with the second a new cartridge was used, produced by J. D. Pedersen, another excellent arms designer, also employed at the Springfield arsenal. In 1932, however, the .276 was definitely abandoned in favour of the .30/06. In 1936 the rifle, greatly improved, was officially adopted and production was begun at the Springfield arsenal.

The **M1 Garand** is a gas-operated semi-automatic rifle. Some of the gas is bled off just after the moment of firing through a small vent in the front of the barrel, near the muzzle, and its pressure operates a piston that ejects the case and reloads the weapon. The Garand, however, can also work as an ordinary single-shot rifle: it was used as such with the addition of a grenade launcher fixed on the barrel.

The Garand is 43.6 inches long without its bayonet and weighs 9.5 pounds; its fixed magazine holds eight rounds in a box magazine housed in the wooden stock; the rear sight is calibrated from 1 to 12 (100–1,200 yards); the bullet has a maximum muzzle velocity of 2,805 feet per second; the maximum range is 3,600 yards; and the rate of fire is from 16 to 24 r.p.m.

Although it is an excellent weapon, with ballistic qualities comparable to those of a machine gun, the M1 Garand still has one drawback in its great weight. It was necessary, therefore, to supply the Army with a lighter all-purpose individual weapon, which would replace pistol, rifle, and sub-machine gun. With this in mind, the American armaments authorities organised a competition in 1940 for a semi-automatic carbine weighing no more than $5\frac{1}{2}$ lbs. The competition was won by the Winchester Repeating Arms Company, one of the best known armourers of the world. Winchester's technicians had prepared the carbine in the record time of 48 days, between the creation of the prototype, tests, and alterations requested by the assessment committee. The weapon was introduced into the Army as the U.S. M1 carbine, and during the war it had ample opportunity to prove its qualities, which, even if not as multi-purpose as they were intended to be, nevertheless earned it considerable respect.

The **M1 Carbine,** like the Garand, is gas-operated. It is different from the rifle, apart from a few technical changes, in its weight, its very compact dimensions, and its cartridge. In fact, although the calibre is the same as that of the rifle, the cartridge, also created by Winchester, is much shorter: about 43 mm. The M1 weighs 5.5 pounds and is only about 35.6 inches long. Accurate sighting is at 300 yards. The maximum range is 2,000 yards and the magazine holds 15 or 30 rounds.

The carbine was also adapted in a different version for assault troops, with a folding metal stock (M1A1), and in one which could fire automatically, in bursts (M2). In the latter the magazine holds 30 rounds.

THE COLT M1911A1 SEMI-AUTOMATIC PISTOL (U.S.A.)

Of all semi-automatic military pistols, the prize for length of service goes undoubtedly to the Colt M1911, which has been in use by the United States Army for more than 60 years. This, more than anything else, is evidence of the effectiveness of this weapon, which has seen service in World War I, World War II, Korea, and Vietnam.

In fact the version used in World War I is slightly different from the one used later, which is known as the **M1911A1**; but the alterations only improve the weapon without affecting its original characteristics.

The Colt M1911 derives from the automatic military pistol in .45 calibre designed by John Moses Browning in 1905 and turned down by American small arms experts because it is too complicated. Browning's new model was tested in 1911, together with other excellent weapons, such as the American Savage and the German Luger, all in .45-inch calibre. This calibre had been stipulated by the Americans as being the only one, according to them, which could guarantee great stopping-power.

The tests were rigorous. The last one, for example, consisted of firing the weapon after it had been cleaned of all its oil and then exposed to acid fumes, which made it rust. The Colt was judged the best of all the arms submitted, and was, therefore, adopted as the M1911. In 1923, after a few alterations to the grip, the weapon was renamed as we have noted, the M1911A1.

The Colt M1911 is a semi-automatic pistol which works on the recoil principle, with barrel and slide recoiling unequal distances (0.05 inches for the first, 2.2 inches the second). Its weight, unloaded, is 2.25 pounds; barrel length is five inches; the magazine contains seven rounds; the bullet, weighing 0.535 ounces, has a muzzle velocity of 830 feet per second. This low velocity, combined with the weight and calibre of this pistol, gives the bullet a very high stopping-power. A shot from a Colt can literally stop a man in his tracks even if he is not fatally wounded, simply by the tremendous impact of the bullet.

◁ Men of the U.S. 77th Infantry Division advance towards Shuri on Okinawa across a spliced-ladder bridge over a gulch. The two leading men are holding .45-inch M1911A1 Colt semi-automatic pistols, the others two M1 rifles and an M1 carbine.

△ Cutaway view of the American M1911A semi-automatic pistol.
▽ The M1911A1 pistol, adopted in 1926 to replace the M1911. The latter does not have a bulged and serrated main spring housing (bottom rear of stock), a serrated trigger, or finger clearance cut-outs on the receiver, behind the trigger.

THE LUGER PO8 & WALTHER P38 (Germany)

During World War I, the German Army's automatic pistol was, besides the Mauser M1912 in 7.63-mm or 9-mm Parabellum calibre, the **Luger M1908** or simply P08 (the "P" is for *Pistol*). The Luger remained the standard pistol of the German Army until 1938, when the Walther P38 was adopted. Even after this date, however, the P08 remained in service, and was manufactured until 1942.

Luger is one of the most respected names in the history of automatic pistols. The story of this weapon began in the United States, where Hugo Borchardt, of the Winchester Repeating Arms Company, in 1893 patented an automatic pistol with unusual characteristics: its breech-block is hinged on a jointed arm which folds upwards at the moment at which the pressure of the gas makes the breech-block recoil. The only other pistol in which one can find this mechanism, which is similar to a human knee-joint and is unique among automatic pistols, is the one designed by George Luger, an engineer of the "Deutsche Waffen und Munitionsfabriken" (D.W.M.), the German factory which, towards the end of the century, produced Borchardt's pistol. Luger reduced the cumbersome proportions of the Borchardt, modified its line, and altered Borchardt's 7.63-mm jacketed, bottle-necked round to take a heavier charge. The new weapon was ready in 1898, under the name Borchardt-Luger "Parabellum", which was inspired by the Latin motto *"si vis pacem para bellum"* (if you want peace prepare for war). It was offered to the armies of many countries and was first adopted, in 1900, by the Swiss. It was subsequently improved and altered in the models of 1906 and 1908. The latter is the most famous of the Luger pistols. It is in 9-mm Parabellum calibre and was made in two versions: one with a 10-cm (4-inch) barrel and fixed sights, and one with a 15-cm (6-inch) barrel, with an adjustable sight calibrated on 100 and 200 metres, and a detachable stock which can be fitted onto the butt so that the pistol can be used as a small carbine. The first version weighs two pounds and has a removable magazine holding eight rounds. During World War I, a later model of the Luger, the M1914, was used alongside the P08, and this has 10-, 15-, or 20-cm (8-inch) barrels. A very popular pistol, the Luger was made in about 30 different versions by arms manufacturers of many different countries, even from spare parts. In 1930, official construction of the Luger was entrusted to the Mauser works at Oberndorf, which supplied to the *Reichswehr* only the M1914 with a 10-cm barrel; from 1938 to 1942 Mauser produced more than 400,000 of them. Production was interrupted when the construction of the new German service pistol, the **Walther M1938** or P38, was well under way.

The Walther P38 is one of the best 9-mm Parabellum calibre weapons ever produced. The most interesting thing about it is that it is a double action weapon—in other words, with the cartridge in the chamber and the hammer lowered, one can fire simply by pressing the trigger, which cocks and then fires the weapon.

The Walther P38 is an adaptation for war of the first efficient double-action semi-automatic pistol, the MPP (Pistol Polizei), produced in short 9-mm calibre in 1929 by Walther for the police. The P38 weighs 2.1 pounds and has a barrel 4.9 inches long. The detachable box magazine holds eight rounds. Its power is considerable: the muzzle velocity of the bullet is around 1,115 feet per second, and the maximum range is around 1,000 yards. From 1938 to the end of the war over a million of them were made.

△ A Gefreiter *(lance-corporal) of the* Panzerwaffe *checks his 9-mm Parabellum Model 08 (Luger 08) pistol.*
▷ *An American soldier shelters in the cover of a doorway in Brest with his captured 9-mm Walther P38 semi-automatic pistol.*
△▷ *A German soldier wades across a section of the Pripet Marshes with his 7.92-mm MP 44 assault rifle.*
▷▷ *German troops learn how to use their 9-mm MP38 submachine guns on an airfield in Norway.*
△▷▷ *German infantryman in action with his 9-mm MP38 submachine gun. The most serious battlefield deficiency of this model was the lack of an adequate safety device, which was rectified on the MP38/40. Another failing was the cost of this well-made weapon, and this was corrected in the MP40, which was basically similar, except for the elimination of the ribbing on the receiver, and the design of the ejector and magazine release assembly.*

THE MP38 SUB-MACHINE GUN & *STURMGEWEHR* M43-44 (Germany)

By the outbreak of World War II the importance of individual light-weight automatic weapons had been fully realised. The effectiveness of such weapons had been tested during the years immediately before the beginning of the greatest war in history: in 1932, during the Chaco War between Bolivia and Paraguay, enormous numbers of Schmeisser MP28II sub-machine guns had been sent to arm the Bolivian Army; and during the Spanish Civil War, Bergmann M34's and Erma EMP's had been supplied by Germany to Franco's troops. And besides these, other models of sub-machine guns, from a variety of European arms manufacturers, had made their presence felt in Spain, in Abyssinia, and in every other part of the world in which fighting broke out. (The German *Maschinenpistole*, or MP, means machine pistol or sub-machine gun.)

German strategy, based on the theory of the swift knock-out blow, depended on the use of large numbers of hand-picked troops to break the enemy's line and strike crippling blows. These troops had to be supplied with light weapons, with a very high rate of fire: the sub-machine gun. The standard German sub-machine guns of the war were the **MP38** and its derivatives, the **MP40II** and the **MP41.**

Many people think that the original design for the MP38 was Hugo Schmeisser's, but authoritative publications attribute it to the engineers of the Erma factory (Erfurt Maschinenfabrik), even though its derivation from the MP18I is certain. The combination of firing-pin and telescopic multi-piece recoil spring was developed from the Erma sub-machine gun; the new weapon, however, did not have the perforated cooling barrel-jacket of previous models. Its great disadvantage, in common with many other sub-machine guns, was an inadequate safety device to prevent accidental firing. An improvement in the safety gave rise to the M38/40 sub-machine gun, or MP38/40.

This model was followed by the M40 sub-machine gun (MP40), the most widely produced sub-machine gun of the 1940–44 period; more than a million were made. The MP40, in 9-mm Parabellum calibre as were all German

sub-machine guns, was an improved version of the MP38, from which it differed in the ejector mechanism, magazine release, and receiver (through which the breech mechanism moves), which had the ribbing eliminated.

The MP40 is a robust weapon, capable of automatic fire only, and measures 28.8 inches with the steel stock folded and 32.8 inches with it extended; the barrel is 9.9 inches long; its weight is 8.15 pounds; its box magazine holds 32 rounds in two staggered rows; and the muzzle velocity of the bullet is around 1,300 feet per second.

One version of the MP40, the MP40II, has provision for two magazines side by side, holding a total of 64 rounds.

We come now to the MP43, which cannot properly be classed as a sub-machine gun. It was a weapon on which the Germans had been working since 1938, and its mechanism was so advanced that after its first appearance and its use by the troops of the Third Reich it influenced development of all infantry armament in the post-war period and up to the present time. The weapon was not intended for special assault troops

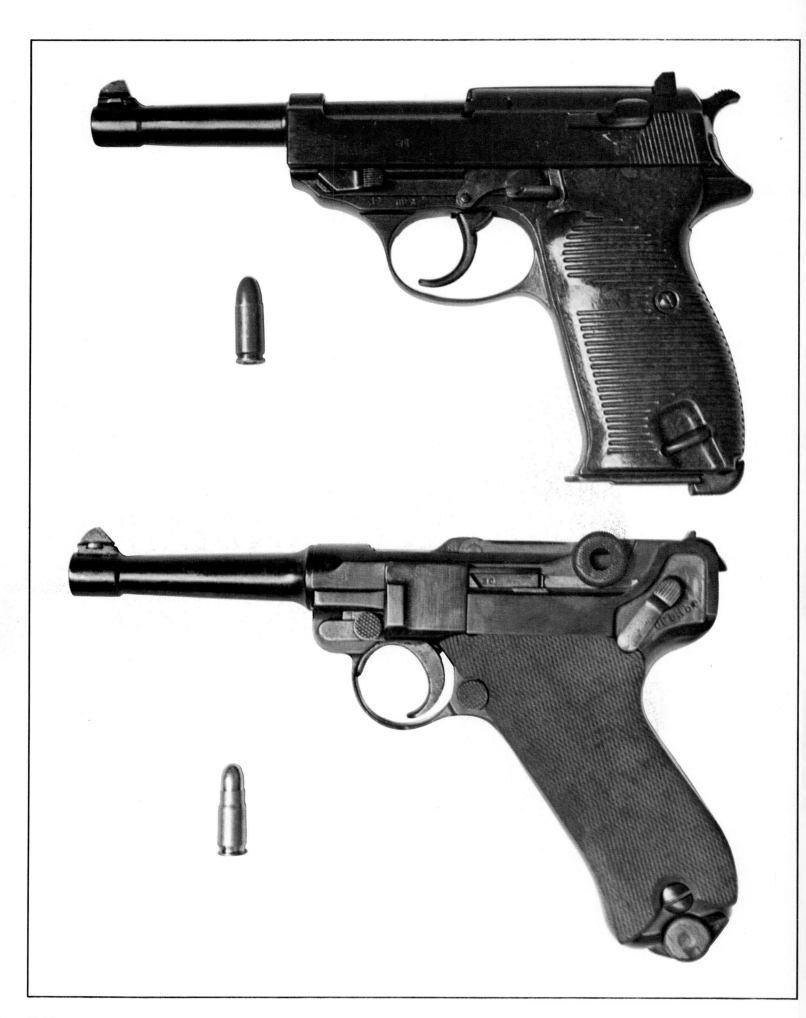

but for the infantry generally, and it had characteristics that made it quite distinct from even the most modern military rifle of the time, the American M1 Garand. It was a short automatic rifle, using the completely new 7.92-mm *Infanterie kurz Patrone* (7.92-mm short infantry cartridge).

The cartridge and ensuing prototype weapons for its use were commissioned in 1938 from two manufacturers, Haenel of Suhl and Polte of Magdeburg. The cartridge was ready two years later, and in 1942 the weapon itself was completed.

Meanwhile, the firm of Walther had also prepared a prototype. The final model, the MP43, was the one from Haenel, but with the firing and percussion mechanisms of the Walther model.

The weapon was called the MP43, possibly for reasons of security, because its manufacture necessitated the use of machines, skilled workers, and raw materials that many people would have preferred to see used for the construction of more conventional weapons. Later, however, when the weapon had proved its efficiency, it was given the definitive designation **Sturmgewehr StG44** (M44 assault rifle).

The StG44 is gas-operated, and not blowback-operated as are previous true sub-machine guns. It is 37 inches long and the barrel measures 16.5 inches. Unloaded it weighs 9.5 pounds and with a full magazine 11.5 pounds. The magazine holds 30 rounds in staggered rows. The rear sight is calibrated in hundreds of metres up to 800 metres. The bullet weighs 8.4 grams and has a muzzle velocity of 2,132 feet per second. Operation is automatic or semi-automatic. The body of the weapon, incorporating the barrel, recoil, and firing mechanism and magazine housing, is made of stamped steel plate, at that time considered revolutionary.

Despite the increasing difficulties, large quantities of the StG44 were distributed to the troops. But this superb weapon could not prevent the fall of Hitler's Germany.

Opposite page, top: *The German 9-mm Walther P38 semi-automatic pistol.*
Opposite page, bottom: *The German 9-mm Parabellum Model 08 (Luger P08) semi-automatic pistol.*
◁ *The German 7.92-mm MG42 machine gun, with the feed cover open. This machine gun was designed to replace the MG34, which was expensive to manufacture as a result of the large number of machined parts. To facilitate production, the MG42 had a large number of stampings incorporated in the design.*
▽ ◁ *An MG42 machine gun team in Russia. The feed of the belt from the left was the responsibility of the crew's No. 2, on the right in the photograph.*
▽ *Twin MG34 anti-aircraft mounting.*

THE MG34 & 42 MACHINE GUNS (Germany)

The story of one of the best machine guns of the world, if not absolutely the best, goes back to the aftermath of the Treaty of Versailles, by which Germany had been forbidden to manufacture heavy machine guns. This limitation, which excluded the traditional Maxim used by the German Army, resulted in the adoption of a lighter model of the Dreyse M1918 machine gun, the MG 13, keeping the 7.92-mm cartridge of the standard rifle. However, this was a makeshift solution, and German arms designers set to work at the end of the 1920's to create a new light machine gun which would have the same properties as the heavy machine gun. Thus, just as Nazism was becoming firmly established as the new ruling power in Germany, there was introduced a machine gun which, while keeping within the limitations of the treaty, left nothing to be envied in weapons of similar calibre in other countries: this was the **MG34.**

The weapon was a product of Rheinmetall and Mauser, and was inspired by guns produced by the Swiss firm of Solothurn. It is in a sense a "machine rifle"–it has a stock which one can rest on one's shoulder and a pistol-grip. It has a slim and compact line and measures 48 inches (barrel 24.6

inches), and weighs 25.6 lbs with bipod. It is recoil-operated and is air-cooled, with a perforated barrel-jacket.

Despite the characteristic reduction in weight and size, the excellent construction and the powerful 7.92-mm cartridge give the MG34 remarkable ballistic qualities. Its normal sights are graduated from 200 to 2,000 metres, but with telescopic sights it has a range of 3,500 metres. It is fed by a 250-round ammunition belt or by a 50-round belt in a drum. It is capable of both single-shot and fully automatic fire, and its cyclic rate of fire varies between 800 and 900 r.p.m.

As the gun is extremely versatile, it can be used in a wide range

△ *The German MG (Maschinengewehr) 34 machine gun. This weapon was designed at the behest of the* Waffen Amt *(Weapons Department) by the celebrated Mauser concern. Well designed and excellently made, the MG 34's chief drawback was its expense. Clearly visible here is the unusual trigger: when it is pulled at the top the weapon fires semi-automatically; when pulled at the bottom, automatically.*

▽ *The German MG42 machine gun. This was designed to replace the MG 34, and is apparently derived from a Polish design captured in 1939. The final design was completed by Dr. Grunow, of Grossfuss in Doblen. The principal distinction of the design is the large scale use of steel stampings to replace the more expensive machined parts typical of the MG 34 design.*

Opposite page, top: *The German* Gewehr 41 (Walther) *semi-automatic rifle. The gas-operated self-loading mechanism is a modification of the Bang system: a cone at the muzzle causes the gas to recoil against a piston, which in turn operates the rod connected to the bolt.*
Centre top: *The German* Gewehr 43 *semi-automatic rifle. This was basically the 41(W) with a Tokarev gas system.*

Opposite page, centre bottom: *The German MP (Maschinenpistole) 40 sub-machine gun. This development of the MP 38 had an improved safety device, and a new magazine housing and receiver.*
Bottom: *The German StG (Sturmgewehr) 44 or MP44 assault rifle. Introduced in 1944, this was intended to replace all the rifles, sub-machine guns, and light machine guns of the army.*

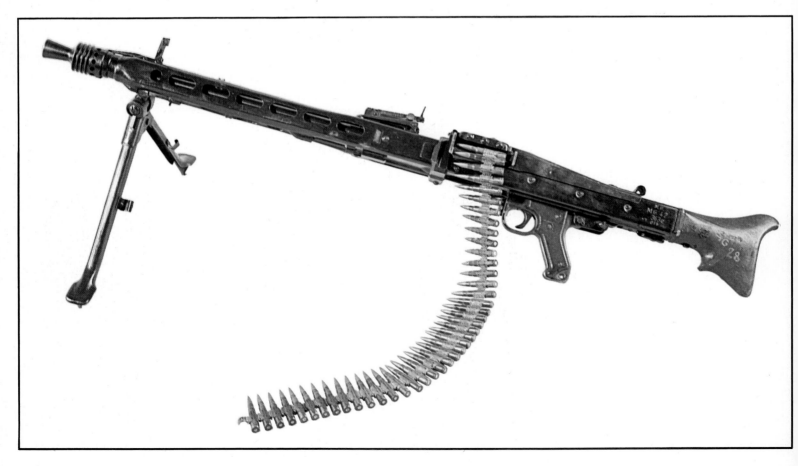

3151

△ *The MG34 in action. Notable design points were a quick-change barrel feature, simple construction (with major components being held together with bayonet catches), a plastic stock, and a combined barrel bearing, recoil booster, and flash suppressor.*

▽ ▷ *German infantry on the move. On the left the soldier is carrying an ammunition box for the machine gun's belts. The man next to him has a 7.92-mm Mauser* Gewehr *98 with a sniper scope, while the man on the extreme right has an ordinary* Gewehr *98. In front of the tree walks a soldier with a drum-fed MG34 machine gun.*

△ ▷ *A German soldier, carrying a* Nebelwerfer *round, approaches a railway flatcar with a 15-cm* Nebelwerfer *41 on it. His personal weapon is a* Gewehr *98.*

▷ ▷ △ *The 7.92-mm* Gewehr *41(M) semi-automatic rifle.*

▷ ▷ ▽ *The 7.92-mm* Gewehr *43 (left).*

of situations: on a bipod it can serve as a light machine gun; on a tripod it is an excellent medium/heavy machine gun; on a suitable high mount it is a perfect anti-aircraft gun.

There is no doubt that a part of the success of the German Army in World War II can be accredited to MG34. However, when Allied resistance strengthened and the illusions of the "lightning war" were shattered, the German war effort was wearing thin. The Wehrmacht asked continually for better weapons, and this demand subjected German industry to such a production race that it had to abandon the mechanical perfection which up till then had been its byword. Arms now had to be less costly and more quickly made, and this specification gave rise to the **MG42,** in 7.92-mm calibre—the best machine gun ever to appear until then on the field of battle.

To speed up and simplify its manufacture, German technicians used stamped steel, a new material then in its early stages. Among other advantages, the use of stamped steel made it possible for any engineering firm, however small, to take part in the production of the weapon. And not only the barrel, but the body, the grip, and the feed and firing mechanisms, were made of stamped steel. The MG42 does not look much different from the MG34,

except that the perforated barrel jacket is square and is made in a single piece with the body of the gun. There are differences, on the other hand, in the mechanism, which is also simplified. The gun works on the recoil principle, and the barrel and bolt recoil different distances. The bolt is locked as its face reaches the rear of the cartridge, and firing follows as a result of the firing pin being driven forward by its momentum. This

permits the elimination of a spring for the firing pin itself and of the secondary firing mechanism. Bolt locking is achieved by two mobile rollers which work on the rear part of the bolt.

Forty-eight inches long, like the MG34, the MG42 only weighs 25.5 lbs with bipod. The muzzle velocity is 2,480 f.p.s.; the ballistic qualities of the MG42 are the same as those of the MG34, and the MG42, which fires only automatically, has an exceptional cyclic rate, theoretically of 1,100–1,200 r.p.m., and in practice 20 rounds per second. For this reason the barrel is designed for easy replacement, to avoid excessive heating. The gun is fed from non-disintegrating metal belts, holding 50 rounds. The belts are usually joined in groups of five, to make 250-round belts.

The battle-field appearance of the MG42 led the Allies to think that they were up against a heavy machine gun, and they were very surprised, when they had the opportunity to study a captured gun, to discover that it was a light weapon which could comfortably be carried by one man, like a sub-machine gun. They tried therefore to imitate it, copying it faithfully but adapting it to their own .30-inch rifle cartridge. But their attempt failed, because this cartridge was a little longer than the Mauser 7.92-mm round, and it was therefore impossible, without a major alteration in the design of the gun, to ensure that the empty cartridge case would be ejected efficiently.

THE *GEW* 41(W) & *GEW* 43 SEMI-AUTOMATIC RIFLES (Germany)

Italy was not the only country to enter into World War II without an efficient semi-automatic, or self-loading rifle, for her infantry. All the other belligerent nations went into the conflict in the same state of unpreparedness, except the United States and Russia.

This may lead one to believe that, all in all, Italy's armaments authorities had behaved much like those of the other nations and therefore that their error of judgement might be considered general. In fact for Italy the story is different, because the problem of producing an individual automatic rifle had been under consideration there since the beginning of the century. In 1908 the Italian Ministry of War had bought a patent from the inventor Filippo Genovesi, dated 1905, for a semi-automatic rifle, using the 6.5-mm calibre of the M1891 rifle. Five hundred examples of this model had been produced in 1911 during the Libyan War, but the results had been disappointing.

In 1911 another semi-automatic rifle, designed by Lieutenant-Colonel Amerigo Cei-Rigotti, was tested, but this again proved unsatisfactory. The fault lay not so much in the weapon itself but in the ammunition: the cartridge of the M91 rifle was unsuitable for use in a simple light-weight mechanism such as was needed in the desired weapon.

It was not until the eve of World War II, when it was decided to change the calibre of Italian infantry weapons to 7.35-mm, that it was possible to make an effective semi-automatic infantry rifle. Such was the M1939 Armaguerra, patented by Gino Revelli, son of the Revelli who designed several semi-automatic weapons at the beginning of the century. But the outbreak of war meant that the ambitious plan to supply this weapon to the Italian Army had to be postponed, as the plan to change the calibre had been shelved.

Nevertheless, some good came out of all this activity: the Cei-Rigotti automatic system. This was the inspiration of the Russians in World War II when they

produced the Tokarev, and of the Germans when, copying the Russian system, they decided that they, too, would produce a semi-automatic infantry rifle. And it is on this principle, finally, that the modern Belgian FN rifle is based, using the standard N.A.T.O. calibre of 7.62-mm.

The Cei-Rigotti has a gas-operated self-loading system. Part of the gas is bled off through a small hole in the barrel, near the muzzle, and its pressure operates a piston on the barrel connected to a piston-rod; this last, moving backwards along the barrel, operates the mechanism that ejects the empty case and reloads.

The Germans, having gone into the war with the Mauser *Gewehr* 98k, an ordinary bolt-action rifle, were not slow to understand the importance of the Russian Tokarev, and set about finding ways of producing an efficient semi-automatic infantry rifle for themselves. Thus they ordered two models of 7.92-calibre rifle: the **Gewehr 1941 (Mauser)** and the **Gewehr 1941(Walther).** These are both gas-operated, with the piston placed below the barrel. The *Gewehr* 41(W) turned out to be better in practice than the Mauser, and was manufactured in large quantities. It is 44 inches long and weighs 11.08 pounds. It has a muzzle velocity of about 2,550 feet per second. The magazine, in the lower part of the stock, holds ten rounds.

The *Gewehr* 41(W), although a good weapon, turned out to be inferior to the Russian and American semi-automatic rifles. Well made, but very delicate, it had also the disadvantage of being very heavy. In 1943, therefore, a new semi-automatic rifle was adopted, inspired by the Tokarev, of whose efficiency the Germans had become all too aware in their long war against the U.S.S.R. With the **Gewehr 1943**, construction methods were reduced to the most basic simplicity. The line of this weapon is different from that of the Mauser 98k, which had been followed until then. The weapon, 44 inches long (barrel 21.62 inches), weighs about 9.5 pounds and is, of course, in 7.92-mm calibre. The piston is on the top of the barrel, as in the Tokarev. The detachable magazine holds ten rounds; and the muzzle velocity is 2,250 feet per second. The *Gewehr* 43 was the most widely produced of the German semi-automatic rifles. (*Gewehr* means rifle, and is often abbreviated to *Gew.*)

THE BREN & STEN GUNS
(Great Britain)

In 1930 the British War Office, wishing to supply its infantry with a light machine gun, put in hand a series of experiments on various types of machine guns, among which were the Danish Madsen (derived from one of the first arms of this kind to appear in the military field), the French Berthier, and the Czech Brno Zb M1927. (The Model 1926 was ordered, but Brno sent the improved Zb 27.) The results of these experiments were entirely in the favour of the Czech model. From the point of view of ballistics and of the quality of the materials from which it was constructed, the weapon proved at once to be so exceptional and so well fitted to British requirements that an immediate order was placed.

In fact the Brno Zb M1927 was one of the best weapons of the type ever made. It had been designed by the brothers Václav and Emanuel Holek, two first-class Czech technicians, with the help of an Austrian and a Polish engineer, Marek and Podradsky. The weapon, in 7.92-mm calibre, is gas-operated, and is capable of automatic and single-shot fire. It is robustly built and well suited to the rigours of use in the field, and is made of excellent materials. The barrel, for example, which is interchangeable, can be cooled in cold water even when red-hot.

When adopting the weapon for their army, the British had a few necessary modifications made, first of all in the calibre, since the cartridge to be used was the standard .303-inch rifle round. They asked also that the barrel be shortened a little, thereby moving the gas block 9.65 inches

nearer the chamber, to reduce cordite fouling. When the changes had been made, the gun was almost 2¼ lbs lighter than the original. The Zb firm produced it for the British as the ZBG.

In 1937, however, Great Britain obtained a licence to start producing it in England, and this task was entrusted to the Royal Small Arms Factory at Enfield—from this the gun took its name, **Bren**, which was made up of the first two letters of the names Brno and Enfield. The first 200 guns were delivered in January 1938. By now the threat of imminent war could no longer be ignored, and production, which in 1938 had reached a rate of 300 guns a week, was accelerated. At the outbreak of war productivity had reached 1,600 guns per month.

There are four different versions of the Bren, which vary only in small details. The Mark 1 and Mark 2 have 25-inch barrels (the barrels of the Mark 3 and Mark 4 are 22.25-inch), and weigh 22.12

and 23.18 lbs respectively. The muzzle velocity with Mark VII ball is 2,440 f.p.s.; and the cyclic rate, from Mark 1 to Mark 4 respectively, is 500, 540, 480, and 520 r.p.m. The curved box magazine holds 30 rounds, but only 28 rounds are loaded normally in order to avoid straining the magazine spring.

One might say that the British Army went into the war with only the Bren as an automatic light weapon. The military authorities did not in fact realise at first the important part that the sub-machine gun would play, and did not adopt it on any large scale. The Lanchester Mark 1, although designed before the outbreak of war on the inspiration of the German MP29II, was only distributed from 1941 onwards, in relatively small quantities, to the Navy. In 1941, however, large-scale adoption of the **Sten** had been decided –the Sten Machine Carbine, as it was officially called. This was a direct result of the defeat at Dunkirk, in which the British had succeeded in carrying their men to safety, but only after most of their weapons had been lost. This necessitated a rearmament programme based on an efficient weapon which could be produced cheaply.

In June 1941 the prototype of the Sten was ready, and the job of producing it was assigned to the B.S.A. (Birmingham Small Arms) and the Royal Ordnance Factory at Fazakerley. In November of the same year the weekly output had reached 2,000. Later on, when production of the Sten had been extended to other firms, it rose to 25,000 guns per week in the second quarter of 1942 and to 47,000 in the following year. Total production, in all the various versions of the weapon, was 3,750,000 between 1941 and 1945. And the average production cost of the Sten in England was only two dollars – the American Thompson cost ten!

The Sten is typical of the blow-back-operated type of sub-machine gun, sacrificing elegance and refinement in the interests of efficiency and ruggedness. The firing mechanism, the breech-block, and the barrel are made of stamped steel. A single large

A A ◁ *The British 9-mm Sten Mark II sub-machine gun.*
A ◁ *Men of the Royal Ulster Rifles during the street fighting for Bremen in April 1945. The two corporals on the left are armed with .303-inch Short, Magazine, Lee Enfield No. 4 Mark 1 rifles. The two light machine guns are .303-inch Bren Mark 2's. The Mark 2 differed from the Mark 1 in having a simplified butt and a leaf rear sight in place of the radial drum-moved aperture type.*
◁ *A Bren gun, mounted on a tripod in the anti-aircraft rôle. Note the special 100-round drum magazine in place of the more usual 30-round box magazine.*
A *Italian partisans, armed with Sten sub-machine guns. Note the number of spare magazines in evidence.*

spring operates the automatic firing mechanism. The heavy cylindrical breech-block has a fixed firing pin and extractor. The selector for automatic fire is conveniently situated below the safety cut-out for the cocking-handle. The box magazine, holding 32 rounds, fits horizontally into a housing on the left: on the other side is the ejector port. The sights are also very simple, calibrated to 100 yards. The calibre is the classic 9-mm. The safety is a cut-out in the return-spring housing, above the cocking-handle slot.

The most widespread version of the Sten is the Mark II, 30 inches long (barrel length 7.75 inches), weighing 6.62 lbs. Muzzle velocity is 1,200-1,280 f.p.s. and cyclic rate 540-575 r.p.m. Over two million of these guns were made between 1942 and 1944, and a fair number was distributed to resistance forces in German-occupied countries. The most common butt for the Sten is made of steel, light-weight and T-shaped. There are versions for special forces, with a silencer (the Mark IIS) and the Mark IV. An almost identical gun was made by the Germans, who were also always on the look-out for simple and efficient weapons.

THE ENFIELD .38 REVOLVER (Great Britain) and BROWNING H.P. M1935 PISTOL (Canada)

The Webley No. 1 Mk. VI, the service revolver supplied to the British Army from 1915 to 1936, is one of the most powerful and robust weapons ever made; its .455-inch calibre, however, is too great for use by anyone who is not sufficiently trained to use it, as is its weight (2.37 pounds). It was decided, therefore, to design a lighter revolver which would fire a smaller cartridge. In 1923, Webley had produced a revolver pistol for the police force, and this proved a good starting point. So, while on one side research was being carried out on a cartridge which, although of a lesser calibre, would retain the stopping power of the .455, the Enfield Royal Small Arms Factory was working on improvements to the Webley 1923 design. The result was the Enfield revolver.

The Enfield fires a .38-inch cartridge at a muzzle velocity of 600 feet per second, and weighs 1.58 pounds (1.48 pounds in the No. 2 Mk. 1* and Mk. 1**). The barrel is five inches long and the cylinder holds six rounds. The Enfield was made in three ver-

sions: the No. 2 Mk. 1, the No. 2 Mk. 1*, and the No. 2 Mk. 1**. The first was adopted in 1936 and is the basic weapon. The second was introduced in 1938 and differs from its predecessor in having no cocking-spur on the hammer. This was done as the weapon was intended for use by tank crews, in whose bulky clothes it was thought the cocking-spur of the basic Mk. 1 would catch. The result is that the weapon can only be used double-action, and is thus almost impossible to fire accurately, so heavy is the action. The third version was introduced in 1942 and has no hammer safety stop, and can only be fired as a double action weapon. Like the Webley, the Enfield is a conventional hinged-frame design.

However, the British Army also needed an automatic pistol. The old World War I Webley semi-automatics remained in use, along with the Browning M1935 "Hi-Power" automatic.

Browning designed the Hi-Power in 1923. The patent for the prototype was registered in 1927, two months before his death. The production of this weapon was only started, however, in 1935, when the "Fabrique Nationale d'Armes de Guerre" (F.N.) of Herstal, Belgium, produced it in two versions: the "ordinary model" with fixed rear sight, and the model with a rear-sight calibrated to 500 metres and a detachable shoulder stock.

Meanwhile, the John Inglis Company of Toronto, Canada, had bought a licence to make the Hi-Power and was producing it for the Canadian Army and for the Allies. This same Browning was supplied to the British troops in large numbers.

The Browning H.P. deserves its name Hi-Power. Built in 9-mm Parabellum calibre (but also in 7.65-mm Luger), its main characteristic, besides the intrinsic power of the cartridge (with muzzle velocities of between 1,000 and 1,500 feet per second), is the fact that its removable magazine holds 13 rounds. With a round in the breech, therefore, it has 14 rounds to fire in quick succession. The automatic mechanism is of the type that has a barrel and a slide recoiling different distances. It weighs 1.9 pounds and has a barrel 4.75 inches long. The designations of the Canadian-produced models are Pistol, Browning, F.N., 9-mm, H.P., No. 1 Mk. 1 and Mk. 1* (calibrated rear sights) and No. 2 Mk. 1 and Mk. 1* (fixed rear sights).

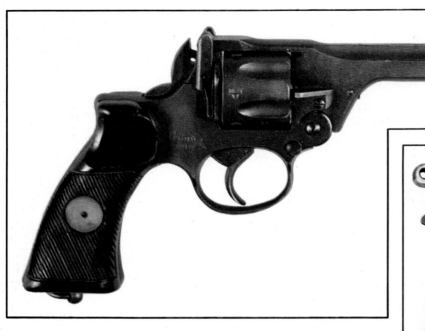

◁ *The British .38-inch Enfield Revolver No. 2 Mark 1*. This differs from the Mark 1 in having no cocking spur on the hammer and is thus double-action.*
▽ *The Belgian 7.65-mm Browning Hi-Power semi-automatic pistol.*

▽ *The British .303-inch Sten Mark II sub-machine gun. Note the safety-device cut-out above the cocking handle slot. When the gun is not in use, the magazine housing can be swivelled round to act as a dust cover for the magazine and ejection ports.*

▽▽ *The British .303-inch Bren Mark 1 light machine gun. Note the radial drum above the pistol grip, used for moving the rear sight, and the wooden carrying handle on the barrel in front of the 30-round curved box magazine.*

THE TT33 PISTOL (Russia)

Even though it bears the Russian name of Tokarev, the semi-automatic TT33 is derived directly from the Colt-Browning M1911. The Tsarist Army had been supplied with one of the most successful revolvers of the end of the 19th Century: the M1895 7.62-mm Mosin-Nagant. This has one main characteristic: its cylinder holds seven rounds instead of six as do most other revolvers.

After the Revolution, however, the Red Army turned its attention to the development of an automatic pistol–although the Nagant M1895 was still being made in 1943. The Russian automatic pistol of World War II was the TT33: the two T's indicate the name of its inventor and that of its manufacturers, the firm of Tula. Like the Nagant, this pistol is in 7.62-mm calibre, which is considered the minimum for a military weapon, even with a high-velocity cartridge.

From the Colt M1911 the TT33 has kept the line, slide stop, and barrel-locking system. The mechanical differences are in the firing and ammunition feed mechanisms. Apart from this, the hammer is not external, as it is in the Colt, but shows only its serrated top above the back of the carriage, along whose central groove it moves. Another distinguishing feature of the TT33 is the lack of safety catch. It can be locked by putting the hammer at half-cock, which blocks the mechanism at about one-third of its travel. It is not one of the safest systems, but it is in line with the Russians' policy of simplifying their weapons to the maximum to allow a fast series production. Crudely made, out of very strong materials, the TT33 is a rough weapon which can function in the most varied conditions of climate and terrain. It weighs 1.88 pounds loaded and has a muzzle velocity of 1,070 feet per second. In emergencies, the Mauser 7.63-mm round can be used. The removable magazine holds eight rounds. Barrel length is 4.57 inches.

THE SVT & PPSh (Russia)

If for Hitler's Germany the Spanish Civil War had been a proving ground for the weapons of future wars, for the Soviet Union, apart from its own experience in that same war, there was the invasion of Finland in 1939. During this brief but bloody conflict, the defects and shortcomings of the Soviet Union's military machine were brought to light. Afterwards the Red Army was purged of its less capable commanders, and a programme of reorganisation was started, which concentrated to a large extent on Soviet weapons, which had proved inadequate for warfare. Most apparent was the need for a semi-automatic infantry rifle, to replace the standard M1891-1930 bolt-action rifle, derived from the Mosin-Nagant, which had been adopted in 1891 by the Tsarist authorities. The Model 1891-1930, in 7.62-mm calibre, was not mechanically different from the original, but was shorter and had a circular instead of a hexagonal barrel. There were substantial changes in the sights and it was given a tangent rear-sight, graduated to a range of 1,000 metres (in the old Mosin-Nagant the ranges were marked in arshins, the Russian unit of measure). It weighed 8.7 lbs, was 48.5 inches long, and had a 5-round magazine.

The Nazi aggression of 1941 caught the U.S.S.R. at the beginning of its reorganisation programme, and so the M1891-1930 rifle remained the basic infantry weapon for the first months of the war, although the Soviet authorities had for some time been working on an efficient semi-automatic infantry rifle. In 1936 this research had produced the 7.92-mm AVS M1936 rifle, which could fire automatically or semi-automatically, but this weapon had proved inadequate and had been abandoned in favour of the semi-automatic **SVT M1938** rifle designed by Fedor V. Tokarev, one of the most brilliant Russian arms designers.

The SVT M1938 is gas-operated and was inspired by the Italian Cei-Rigotti, as are many semi-automatic rifles. It has a wooden butt and a pierced barrel-jacket, part wood and part steel. It has a compensator, a gadget fixed to the end of the barrel to divert the gasses as they issue from the barrel and thus diminish the effect of the recoil. The removable magazine holds ten rounds. The gun is 48.1 inches long and the

barrel measures 25 inches; it weighs 10.8 lbs with bayonet and magazine, and its muzzle velocity is 2,519 f.p.s.; it has a tangent rear sight graduated from 100 to 1,000 metres.

The SVT 1938 was manufactured up to 1940, until another more robust model, the **SVT M1940**, was accepted. This is more suited to military use and does not differ much from the basic model: it weighs 9.48 lbs, and the

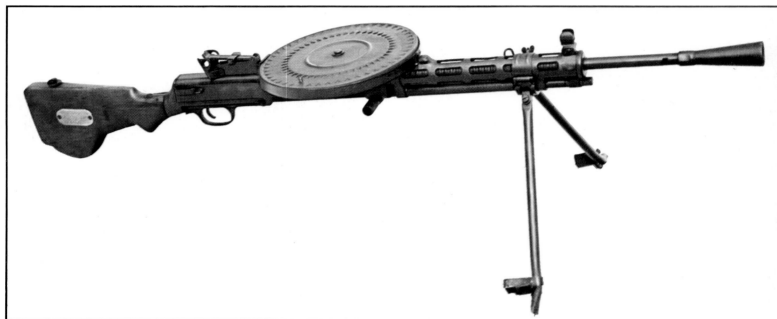

△ ◁ *The Russian 7.62-mm Tokarev Model 1940 SVT semi-automatic rifle. Despite trouble with the flimsiness of earlier models of semi-automatic rifles, the SVT still proved to be too delicate for large-scale use.*

◁ *The Russian 7.62-mm Model 1928 DP light machine gun. The lightweight drum magazine holds 47 rounds.*

▽ ◁ *Russian infantry in action near Orel in 1943. The man nearest the camera has a 7.62-mm Mosin-Nagant Model 1891/30 bolt-action rifle, while to his left another soldier gives covering fire from his DP light machine gun.*

△ *The Russian 7.62-mm Model 1941 PPSh sub-machine gun.*
▷ *The Russian 7.62-mm Tokarev TT Model 1933 semi-automatic pistol. By Western standards, the calibre and power of the round are small.*
▽ *The Russian 7.62-mm Maxim Model 1910 SPM heavy water-cooled machine gun. Note the massive wheeled mounting, which weighs 99.71 pounds with a small armoured shield. The gun itself weighs 52.47 pounds with cooling water.*

barrel length is 24.6 inches. This weapon was the most widely used by the Red Army during World War II and was distributed to officers.

In the course of the war, taking into consideration the results obtained by assault troops with automatic rifles, the Russians abandoned the task of supplying their infantry with semi-automatic rifles, and concentrated on mass producing the sub-machine gun. These were distributed to Guards regiments which in contrast with British practice, were not élite troops but troops which had distinguished themselves on the field of battle. The most common sub-machine gun in the Red Army was the **M1941** or **PPSh 1941**. (The letters "Sh" are for the designer, Georgi Shpagin.) As the pistol cartridge used in the Red Army was the 7.62-mm Tokarev round, the PPSh was designed for the same calibre.

This sub-machine gun is an excellent example of mechanical and structural practicality. All the parts requiring hand-finishing have been eliminated, and the weapon is made of stamped steel, often using barrels taken from old guns, cut in half and chromium-plated to reduce wear. It has no safety, but accidental firing is difficult because the trigger cannot be operated without considerable pressure.

The PPSh 1941 is blowback-operated; the stock is made of wood and the weapon takes two kinds of magazine, a 71-round drum or a 35-round box. It is 33.15 inches long and its barrel measures 10.63 inches; it weighs 11.99 lbs loaded with the drum magazine and 9.26 lbs with the box magazine; it has a tangent leaf or L-type rear sight calibrated from 100 to 200 metres, and the muzzle velocity of the bullet is 1,640 f.p.s. Its range is 200 metres.

THE MAXIM SPM M1910 & DP M1926 MACHINE GUNS (Russia)

As with most nations, if not all, for Russia the history of the

△▷ Swearing-in ceremony for the 77th and 78th Regiments of the Polish Home Army. The machine gun in the foreground is an SPM.
▷ Members of a partisan band in the Kiev area, all equipped with automatic weapons. Among them are two DP light machine guns and eight PPSh sub-machine guns.

machine gun starts with the name of Maxim. In 1902, in fact, the Tsarist Army ordered weapons from the Vickers' Son & Maxim Machine Gun Company. Three years later, the Russian arsenals at Tula were ready to start a massive production of these weapons, to assure adequate supplies to the army. The machine gun produced at Tula was the PM M1905 (the P stands for *palumet*–machine gun– and the M for Maxim). It used the same 7.62-mm cartridges as the standard rifle and it had the classic efficiency and ruggedness of the Maxim system.

In the years immediately before World War I the Russians prepared a new model, the **SPM 1910**, which was different from the first in that the barrel jacket was made of steel instead of bronze. The M1910 was not only used during World War I, but was kept as an infantry machine gun throughout World War II.

The characteristics of the SPM M1910 are much like those of the corresponding Maxim guns adopted by other countries. It works on the recoil principle with a toggle-lock on the breech-block; it is fed by a webbing ammunition belt holding 250 rounds; it is 43.6 inches long (barrel length 28.4 inches), and weighs 52.47 lbs without mount. Theoretically the cyclic rate is 500-600 r.p.m., and the muzzle velocity is 2,822 f.p.s. with a light ball.

The SPM M1910 has two kinds of mounts, both wheeled; the most common, named after its inventor, Sokolov, has a characteristic U-shaped trail, and there are often also two folding feet which, together with the trail, can be stuck into the ground to make a

tripod. The SPM M1910 is capable of single-shot or fully automatic fire, and it remained practically unchanged throughout the 35 years in which it was in service with the Russian Army. The barrel-jacket was changed slightly, being ribbed instead of smooth, and in the final version the hole through which the cooling water was poured was enlarged to permit speedier filling.

As a light automatic weapon the Russian Army produced an indigenous design, the DP M1926. Before starting mass production of the DP, the Russians had tried to make a lighter version of the Maxim, but the results were disappointing, and in fact these weapons were eventually exported to Spain, during the Civil War, and to China.

The **DP M1926** machine gun was a creation of Vassili Alekseevich Degtyarev, a very capable technician, who had been working on it from 1920 to 1921. It was adopted in the late 1920's, and was

mass produced from 1935 onwards under the designation DP M1928. It has a horizontal drum magazine as in the Lewis gun, and is gas-operated, with the peculiar Frijberg-Kjellman locking system. The magazine, which in the Lewis gun turns as it fires, remains static on the DP, with only the interior rotating. It has a bipod and a conical flash suppressor.

In 7.62-mm calibre, and therefore using the standard cartridge the DP M1926 is 50 inches long (barrel 23.8 inches) and weighs 26.23 lbs; the magazine holds 47 rounds, and the tangent leaf rear-sight is calibrated from 100 to 1,500 metres; the muzzle velocity is 2,756 f.p.s. and the rate of fire is around 550 rounds per minute.

In 1944, the gun was altered slightly: the bipod was made more stable, and the recoil spring was moved backwards a little from under the barrel to behind the breech.

△ *The Italian 6.5-mm Breda Model 1930 machine gun. The 20-round box magazine is not detachable, and has to be loaded from chargers. To do this the magazine is folded forward along the barrel.*
▷ *Italian partisans with their motor transport, complete with rifles, sub-machine guns, and a machine gun on the roof.*
▽ *The Italian 8-mm Breda Model 1937 machine gun, mounted on a tripod. The box contains 300 rounds of ammunition, which was fed into the gun in 20-round strips.*

▷ *Italian partisans, armed with British and Italian weapons. The three on the left have Sten submachine guns, and the one on the right a 9-mm Beretta Model 1938A sub-machine gun. In front of them is a Breda Model 1930 machine gun.*
▽ *More partisans. The man on the left appears to be using a 7.35-mm Model 1938 carbine.*
▷ ▷ *A Yugoslav partisan in Slovenia. He is armed with a captured Italian Breda Model 30 machine gun.*
▽ ▷ *Japanese infantry, armed with 6.5-mm Arisaka Type 38 rifles.*

THE BREDA M1930 MACHINE GUN & THE BREDA M1937 MACHINE GUN (Italy)

In the history of Italian weapons, a great many mistakes have been made because Italian arms designers and politicians have had ideas for weapons ahead of their time. There have been many lost opportunities, or at least opportunities not exploited as they should have been. Italy was the first country to realise the virtues of a lightweight automatic assault weapon using ammunition designed for an automatic pistol (the twin-barrelled Revelli Villar Perosa); but she was also the nation which made least use of the machine gun in World War II. Immediately after World War I the Italians, convinced of the necessity of providing their infantry with a light and easily-handled machine gun, or sub-machine gun as it came to be called, graduated from the Fiat M1926 to the Fiat M1928, and on to the Breda 5C, one of the first automatic weapons to have a replaceable barrel, at the time a fairly advanced concept. However, the Breda 5C has a few drawbacks which were not acceptable in a really modern weapon: a grip handle and the need to lubricate each cartridge as it enters the chamber. Moreover, it is mounted on a tripod, and this impairs its manoeuvrability.

In the next version, the M1929, two of these defects were corrected: the gun is fitted with a bipod attached to the barrel and a straight pistol-type stock instead of the grip-handle variety. Finally, in the **M1930**, the pistol stock is slanted to allow a more natural grip. The mechanics of this wea-pon, with their good and bad points, remained unchanged in all three models, as was the calibre (6.5-mm) and the ammunition (that of the M1891 rifle).

The advantage of the Breda M1930 can be summed up simply: it is a well-made weapon. Its disadvantages lie in its delicate mechanism—if it is not properly oiled it can jam easily; in the need for each cartridge to be lubricated as it enters the chamber; in the magazine, which can easily be knocked out of shape and therefore cannot be fitted into the weapon; and in extremely high production costs for a military weapon. Besides these faults there are the small calibre and the low rate of fire, which is no more than 150 rounds per minute.

The Breda M1930 is characterised by its delayed blowback action, the barrel and the breech-block recoiling unequal distances; 6.5-mm calibre; a folding lateral magazine, with 20-round chargers; an air-cooled barrel with steel cooling fins; overall length of 48.5 inches; weight of 22.75 pounds; muzzle velocity of 2,063 feet per second; a maximum range of 3,000 yards; and an effective range of 1,100 yards.

As the M1930 was not up to the standard necessary for use in different climates and terrains, the Italian Government, looking for a replacement for the outdated Revelli (Fiat) M14/35 heavy machine gun, in 1937 adopted the best Italian automatic weapon of World War II; the 8-mm **Breda M1937** machine gun, which uses the same cartridge as the Fiat.

The weapon had been designed four years earlier. From the first it proved itself right for the use for which it was intended—supporting infantry in defence and attack.

For the first time, with the Breda M1937, the Italian Army had an Italian-originated and Italian-built gas-operated, rather than blowback-operated, weapon. Its barrel is air-cooled; fire automatic only; overall length 50 inches; weight 42.8 pounds (the tripod weighing 41.5 pounds); muzzle velocity 2,600 feet per second; rate of fire 450 rounds per minute in theory, 200 in practice; effective range 900-1,100 yards and maximum range 5,900 yards; and ammunition feed from 20-round strips. The barrel can fire 20,000 rounds before it has to be replaced.

The Breda M1937 has a compact and modern line. It needs little maintenance, and can be lubricated either with Breda oil or with olive oil. Its roughness and toughness make it a very reliable weapon, whether in the snows of the Russian steppes or in the sands of the Western Desert. The only points against it are its weight, as compared with the machine guns of other nations, and its low rate of fire.

After the war the Breda M1937 (which was also made in a smaller version for use in tanks) was kept in service, and it was only recently that it was replaced by the German MG 42/59, chambered for the 7.62-mm N.A.T.O. cartridge.

THE M91-38 (Italy) & ARISAKA M38 (Japan) RIFLES

On November 22, 1963, in Dallas, Texas, President John F. Kennedy was killed by three rifle shots. Apart from the sensation caused by the news, one particular aspect of the assassination bemused the weapons experts. According to the Warren Report, the assassin fired a surplus Italian Army rifle, the **M91-38**.

The M91-38 was never very highly thought of–indeed, according to an American catalogue published in 1959, one of these rifles was sold in the United States for only $20. This low price was shared only by the Japanese Arisaka M1905 rifle and was $2 more than the Russian M1891 Mosin-Nagant: all the other military rifles in the catalogue were much more expensive, even the Austrian M1895 Mannlicher.

However, the M91-38 rifle and carbine were undoubtedly good weapons since, while maintaining the simple and rugged qualities of their predecessor, the M91 rifle and carbine, they were yet more robust and handy.

After World War I many nations endeavoured to put their recent experiences to good use and produce improved individual armament. In Italy, however, despite the régime's warlike propaganda, hardly anything was done. In 20 years, from 1918 to 1938, the only new development was the M91-24, which is nothing more than an adaptation of the M91 with the characteristics of the TS carbine of the war period. The only real difference is in the sights, which are identical to the ones in the rifle but calibrated from 600 to 1,500 metres.

Then in 1938 the new model appeared, a fruit of the labours of the arms designer Roberto Boragine. Mechanically similar to the M91, the M91-38 differs from it by its calibre, increased to 7.35-mm; its reduced length (40.2 inches as against 50.8); its rear sight, fixed at 300 metres; and its weight, 7.5 lbs instead of 8.6. At the same time a TS carbine was brought out (for Special Troops), and a cavalry carbine. To increase the calibre, the rifling, whose twist increased towards the muzzle in the 6.5-mm weapon, was left constant in the 7.35-mm. A substantial change was in the bayonet, which was shortened and fixed so that it could be folded back on the handle, permanently attached to the barrel.

However, the decision to adopt a new rifle came too late. At the outbreak of war it was clear that Italy would not be able to produce enough ammunition in 7.35-mm calibre; and the M91-38 rifles were made in 6.5-mm calibre to make them uniform with the M91. Later on in the war the M1941 was adopted: this was virtually a shortened version of the M91.

Of all the belligerent nations of World War II, Italy and Japan were the only ones who did not use automatic or semi-automatic guns widely. Like the Italian, the Japanese soldier went to war with only an ordinary bolt action rifle. The Japanese rifle was the **Arisaka M38** (the 38 corresponds to the year 1905, the 38th year of the Meiji dynasty–the rifle is also known as the M1905). Like the Italian Carcano, the Japanese Arisaka is also in 6.5-mm calibre. The quality materials with which it was built, and its perfect mechanism made it an excellent weapon, but, like the Italian model, it was old-fashioned. It is 50.2 inches long and weighs around 9.25 lbs. The magazine is fitted into the body and is of the Mauser type. The bullet weighs 9 grams and has a muzzle velocity of 2,400 f.p.s. In 1939 the Japanese also decided to increase the calibre of their rifles and produced the M99 or M39. The calibre chosen was 7.7-mm, equal to the British .303-inch, and the bullet, weighing 11.34 grams, has a muzzle velocity of 2,600 f.p.s. It is therefore more powerful than the 6.5-mm.

Whilst on the subject of Japan one must not fail to mention the Type "I" rifle, which has the interesting characteristic that it uses a Carcano breech-block like the M91. It is a 6.5-mm calibre rifle, made on order in Italy for Japan between the end of 1938 and 1939, In all 60,000 of them were made, but it is not known where or when they were used.

THE BERETTA SUB-MACHINE GUN (M.A.B.) M1938/A and M1938/A-1942 (Italy)

The first sub-machine guns (*moschetti automatici* or M.A.) appeared towards the end of World War I. The light two-barrelled Villar Perosa, or Fiat M1915, machine gun was the forerunner of the sub-machine gun, inasmuch as it was the first to use pistol-power ammunition. But, whereas the Villar Perosa was not by definition an assault weapon–although fitted with a sling, its great weight impaired its speed and efficiency– the sub-machine gun, as it had developed by the end of the war, had all the lightness and handiness that made it the new weapon *par excellence* for assault detachments.

The Italian sub-machine gun at the end of World War I was a direct descendant of the twin-barrelled Villar Perosa. It had been arrived at, in fact, by using one barrel of the Revelli machine gun fitted to a rifle stock. The necessary alterations to the new weapon were made by Tullio Marengoni, an engineer from the Beretta arms company of Gardone Valtrompia. This sub-machine gun, although not officially adopted by the Italian Army, was the first of a series that Beretta supplied to Italy's armed forces.

The next model of the Beretta was the M.A.B. 1918-30, a selective fire weapon which like its predecessor used the 9-mm Glisenti cartridge. It is still used by the Italian forest rangers. In 1935 another model was issued, which was fully automatic and which, modified slightly by Tullio Marengoni, led to the creation of the prototype for the 1938 model. The new sub-machine gun was of 9-mm Parabellum calibre; it had two triggers, one for firing bursts, the other for firing single shots; the barrel could be fitted with lugs on which a bayonet with a folding blade could be fixed.

A few minor alterations, such as the addition of a four-slotted compensator, and variations in the line of the stock, resulted in the **M1938/A**, for which Beretta had an immediate order. The first 500 of these sub-machine guns were sent to arm the Italian colonial police in Africa. These, like a large number of their successors, had a fixed bayonet that could be folded back along the barrel.

The M1938A sub-machine gun is a 9-mm calibre weapon, chambered for the Fiocchi M1938 cartridge, which is so similar to the 9-mm Parabellum that the two cartridges are interchangeable,

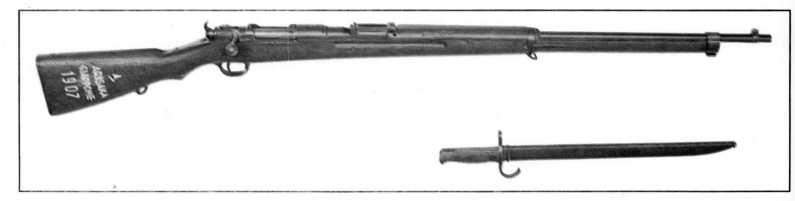

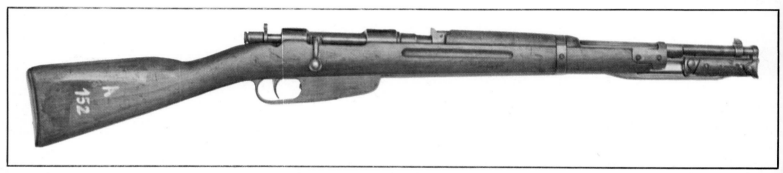

△ *The Japanese 6.5-mm Type 38 (Model 1905) rifle. Experience in the Chinese war showed the Japanese that the 6.5-mm round was not powerful enough, and in 1939 the new 7.7-mm Type 99 rifle was introduced.*

▽ *The Italian 6.5-mm Mannlicher Carcano Model 1891/1938 rifle. Examples built between 1938 and 1940 used the more powerful 7.35-mm round, but after 1940, the 6.5-mm cartridge was readopted.*

▽ ▽ *The Italian Beretta 9-mm Parabellum Model 1938A sub-machine gun. This, with the improved Model 1938A/42, were unquestionably the best Italian small arms of the war, well made and with good performance.*

▽ ▽ ▽ *The Italian Beretta 9-mm Parabellum Model 1938A/42 sub-machine gun. This differed from the 1938A in having a fixed firing pin and an unjacketed barrel. In addition, greater use is made of stampings.*

although the former is rather less powerful than the latter. The M1938/A works on the blowback principle, with a fixed barrel: only the breech-block recoils, under the pressure of the gas on firing, ejecting the spent cartridge case, re-cocking the firing pin, and loading a fresh round

into the chamber. It, too, has two triggers. It is 37.25 inches long (barrel 12.4 inches), and weighs 9.25 pounds. Magazines of 10, 20, 30, or 40 rounds can be used, and it has a rear sight calibrated to 300 metres. The protective barrel-jacket has holes cut in it.

The next model, the **M1938/A-**

1942 (or more precisely 1943), differs from the last on several points; the barrel is shortened to 8.4 inches; the barrel-jacket has been removed; it can have a single sight calibrated on 100 metres, or a blade rear sight calibrated to 200 metres; it weighs 7.2 pounds (the M1938A/1943 7 pounds); and

is 31.5 inches long. The muzzle velocity of the bullet is 1,250 f.p.s.

The production of the various models of M.A.B. was delayed at the beginning of World War II, and therefore the first were ready only in 1942, when they were distributed to special detachments. After September 8, 1943,

CHAPTER 183

Logistics: supplying the American fighting man

Previous page: *A heavily laden L.S.T. approaches Hollandia before the landings on April 22, 1944. She is carrying trucks, jeeps, stores, and water trailers. The vehicles are loaded so that they can be driven straight off to the supply dumps.*
△ *The first stage in the supply chain; a 90-mm anti-aircraft gun is test-fired in the United States. Note the crew includes two women production workers.*
△▷ *Women drivers with a difference: a M3A5 "General Lee" medium tank is driven to the Aberdeen Testing Ground, Maryland, in July 1942. With many men drafted into the services, women became increasingly responsible for the production of munitions, the first stage of the supply pipeline.*
△▷▷ *The real pipeline in the D-Day logistics, P.L.U.T.O., the oil and fuel pipeline stored ready for towing across the Channel on a huge drum. Some 200 miles of pipe are shown in this picture.*
▽▷ *In preparation for the invasion of southern France in August 1944, a vast fleet of all types of craft assembles in a port in southern Italy. It includes tankers, freighters, transports, and warships.*

The science of logistics has seen rapid growth in the 20th Century. In earlier years, when an army would rely on looting or foraging for its supplies in enemy territory, the "administrative tail" contained few technicians or specialists. On the contrary, its camp followers merely supplied some of the troops' immediate needs and gleaned the pickings of a victorious army.

The introduction of gunpowder, and with it artillery and engineer trains, brought a change in the nature and content of the rear echelons, but weapons with a higher rate of fire and the need for greater self-sufficiency marked the real break. Steam ships and locomotives, and finally the internal combustion engine, brought supplies from depots right up to the soldier in the front line.

The static lines in World War I made these supply operations relatively simple, but the ammunition expenditure reached staggering figures. In the first seven days of the Battle of the Somme, the British fired four million shells. In addition, men had to be sent "up the line", fed, and then evacuated either as casualties or when their regiment was withdrawn. By the end of the war Allied staff had begun to work on the problems of mobile war, but these were to be magnified in World War II.

The Americans had some experience of sending men and equipment abroad in large numbers during World War I. But in World War II they were to send huge amounts of equipment to their allies throughout the world as well as troops to Europe, Africa, Burma, China, and the Pacific.

Logistics were a science which was never strictly defined, for at what point does a soldier cease to be part of the support and supply chain and become a fighting man?

Strictly, the man who is loaded up with ammunition or stores as he marches the last few miles to the front is part of the logistic chain. This may seem an extreme example, but the British distinction between "tooth" and "tail" arms rankles on an engineer or signaller who is up front with the infantry.

"Logistics" was and remains a word used by the staff planner, for whom it serves as a convenient symbol to apply to whatever combination of non-combatant activities which happens to be under consideration at that moment.

Military and civilian interaction

Logistics have often been likened to "the military element in the nation's economy and the economic element in its military operations". So there is an interaction between the military and the civilian realms, one demanding and the other producing the three essentials of an army at war.

△ An L.S.T. noses up to a shattered quay at Anzio in January 1944. Its cargo is largely composed of 2½-ton trucks loaded with shells.

▷ Rolling stock, shipped from the U.S.A. to Britain, and thence to France, is off-loaded from a Coast Guard-crewed L.S.T. The French railways had lost most of their rolling stock in Allied air attacks and German demolitions.

▷ △ Troops of the U.S. 5th Army unload mixed stores from a British-crewed landing ship at Anzio in March 1944.

▷ ▷ Like a line of tethered animals, 20 L.S.T.s pour men and equipment ashore at Tacloban airstrip on Leyte in October 1944. Temporary causeways, bulldozed out to the bow doors of the ships, take the vehicles to a makeshift park inland.

They are the means to live (food, water, clothing, shelter, and medical supplies), to move (vehicles, transport animals, fuel, and forage) and to fight (weapons, defences stores, and expendables of ammunition). Some of these items can be used and issued again.

The U.S. Army made a stricter classification of its needs:

1. subsistence and forage;
2. equipment and other items issued to organisations and individuals on the basis of allowance tables;
3. fuels;
4. equipment and materials of irregular issue; and
5. ammunition.

Of these, food and fuel made up the bulk of resupply and replacement needs. Though the rations for one man for a day weighed about six pounds, an army of 50,000 men could consume 4,000 tons of food in a month. However, in the world's most mechanised army, fuel consumption was almost 80 per cent of the resupply

expendables.

Mechanisation meant that the U.S. Army used a lower tonnage of "fuel" than those armies which still relied on animals for their transport. Mules and horses need fodder even while they are resting (the standard grain and hay ration in the 19th Century was 25 lbs per day per animal), but a truck can be parked with an empty tank.

Where the army saved on fuel, it added to its load with ammunition. In the Atlanta campaign of 1864 Sherman estimated that the average ammunition needs of his men were a pound a day, with three pounds on rations.

In World War II average ammunition requirements were 14 per cent of the total resupply and replacement needs, and 21 per cent of the expendables. Replacement of equipment and other non-expendables absorbed only 13 per cent of total resupply and replacement requirements.

The increase in ammunition expenditure can be explained by the high rate of fire of American weapons and also by the larger numbers carried in a division. An infantry division of 15,000 men had 328 guns, while an armoured division had some 1,000 guns. In addition, these weapons had a variety of calibres, ranging from the 50-inch heavy machine gun fitted to the cabs of trucks or the turrets of tanks, to the towed 155-mm howitzers.

Awkward administrative basis

A military unit, be it a patrol of a dozen men, or an army group plunging through a continent, is restricted by three elements –power, mobility, and range.

The patrol can carry most of its short term needs, but a larger group must have depots and bases. If there is a steady supply from these depots the group can incorporate all three elements.

△ ◁ *The classic amphibious combination. British soldiers with American D.U.K.W.s and landing craft. The D.U.K.W. could be used as a lighter to ferry stores from off-shore ships to the invasion beach.*
◁ ◁ *Two Italian civilians assist U.S. soldiers unload 155-mm shells from a D.U.K.W. The picture was taken in February 1944 at Anzio, when the Germans were counter-attacking the Allied beach-head.*
△ *In an attempt at self-sufficiency, a 105-mm M7 tows a trailer loaded with stores. The vehicle is also slung with packs and crates. Despite these precautions, some tanks and self-propelled guns outran their wheeled stores and fuel supplies.*
◁ *Even truck crews enjoyed the victors' triumph. Here trucks of the 2nd Armoured Division drive through the Place de l'Etoile on August 25, 1944.*

3172

Clearing and restoring the supply lines was a very important feature of the support operations behind the front.

◁◁ *Under cover of a smoke screen a 1½-ton truck and a jeep are rafted across the Moselle in 1944.*

▽ ◁◁ *Road building in a Leyte swamp. While bulldozers push a road through the jungle in the background, engineers construct a timber and sand-bag bridge.*

◁ *July 1944. An Osgood shovel loads rubble from ruined houses in the French town of La Haye du Puits.*

▽ ◁ *A 2½-ton truck and trailer cross a pneumatic pontoon bridge in northern France. The shattered and twisted spans of the canal road bridge testify to the destructive skills of the German engineers.*

The last days of the war: a sign writer adds the final touches to the Truman Bridge name board for the pontoon bridge over the Elbe. Such light-weight and quickly-assembled bridges made major rivers like the Seine, the Rhine, and the Elbe no obstacle to determined engineers. Pontoons could be towed across to the far bank as soon as it was reasonably secure and building began on both banks. With practice and experience units could assemble a bridge at very short notice.

In order to build up stocks for each theatre, the U.S. Army developed an elaborate administrative process.

Requirements were calculated by major items and groups of items for the whole army, on the basis of general expectations as to its composition, rate of expansion, and overseas employment, and in the areas in which it would operate. Requirements were grouped under the following headings:

1. initial equipment for each soldier that the army expected to mobilise;
2. replacement equipment to cover the expected losses in use and in combat, as indicated by the analysis of past experience;
3. consumption and expenditure requirements for expendable supplies, also based on past experience; and
4. distribution requirements for both equipment and supplies needed to fill the pipeline in the army's world-wide system of supply, and thus ensure ready availability when and where needed.

Reserves were also built up to cover unforeseen needs. Long-term schemes to deal with other such eventualities as might arise during campaigns were also attempted.

As can be seen, this system aimed to anticipate estimated demand, rather than fulfill needs as they arose in the field. It was a wasteful system, but more economical than one which relied on calculated oversupply.

The British system superior?

In 1942 the British had tried to persuade the Americans to adopt their system, which calculated requirements theatre by theatre on the basis of projected deployment and predicted intensity of combat in each area. Integration of supply systems would mean that they could be administered by a joint staff. But there was some suspicion by the Americans that this system might syphon off the bulk of supplies for forces in theatres occupied by the British and so starve the new American forces.

This consideration weighed more heavily with influential American plan-

ners than the defects of their system. In 1945 General Patrick Tansey, Chief of the Operations Division, War Department Logistics Group during a large part of the war, concluded that the British system was superior to that adopted by the U.S. Army. However, it could not have been used in 1942 because of the "existence of the present form of munitions assignments machinery".

The British had committed the bulk of their forces abroad by 1942, and consequently knew the strengths of their forces in various theatres, but the Americans were still building up their army. Any predictions as to the timing, scale, and direction of its eventual overseas deployment might not fit in with American strategic plans yet to be prepared.

America's capacity to mass-produce weapons was unrivalled during the war, but while she could manufacture the goods, the difficulty was whether they could be delivered. In 1942 and early 1943 German U-boats still dominated the Atlantic sea-lanes. Though from the latter part of 1942 sinkings were outstripped by the production in U.S. shipyards, the

△ *In a depot near Cherbourg, a M29 carrier ploughs through thick mud caused by the November rains. The M29 "Weasel" was originally built for use in snow, but here gives a good performance in different terrain. General Eisenhower was to comment that all his commands, in North Africa, Italy, France, and Germany, were dogged by bad weather.*
◁ *The much maligned M.P.: military police on early morning duty in Venafro in Italy. They were a vital part of the supply system, keeping the traffic moving to and from the front, and preventing pilfering of supplies by soldiers and civilians.*

3176

◁ ◁ *Squeezed into the back of their ¾-ton trucks, men of a 75-mm pack howitzer battery move through the snow in Belgium in 1945.*

▽ ◁ ◁ *A military policeman stands on a nearly submerged cable drum as he directs vehicles on a muddy road on the French border with Germany. America's mechanised army saved the soldier from a back-breaking march from a rail-head to the front.*

◁ *A stockpile of rations in the Pacific in the early years of the war.*

▽ ◁ *Rations and their consumers, the final destination of the logistic chain. Marines of the 3rd Marine Division get their first hot meal at a "chow line" on Guam in July 1944.*

Transport variations.
◁ ◁ In the early days of the war a jeep is off-loaded from a Dakota in Northern Ireland. An aircraft of unusual versatility, the Dakota became one of the major transport aircraft of the war.
▽ ◁ ◁ At the other end of the transport scale, man-power. A section of men with ammunition boxes attached to pack frames plods up an Italian mountain north of Venafro. In this sort of country, men or mules were the only practicable form of transport.
◁ Captured transport: G.I.s unload a truck which was once part of a Flakabteilung. Though the Americans had less need of captured vehicles, there was still a social cachet for some officers who possessed a Kübelwagen.
▽ ◁ A wounded German officer is helped from a captured Sd.Kfz. 251 half-track serving as an extempore ambulance. A group of U.S. corpsmen wait to assist the prisoner, taken in the fighting in Chambois.

△ *Not all the traffic in the logistic pipeline flowed from bases to the front. This man, seriously wounded in fighting in the Pacific, is laid gently on the ground at the beginning of the journey back to a hospital ship. The classification of corpsmen, signallers, or engineers as support troops in the rear echelons was a galling over-simplification of their work. There was always a substantial number of these men in the front line taking risks as great as, and sometimes greater than, the combat infantryman.*

convoying, circuitous routes, and scheduling constituted a bottleneck in overseas deployment more restrictive than the shortage of shipping itself.

The *matériel* did get through, however, and this was of immense significance for the Allies and their prosecution of the war. Churchill said that because of the military aid they received, the British were able to fight as though they were a nation of 58 million instead of 48 million.

The new French armies of 1944, composed of their North African forces, were almost entirely armed and equipped from U.S. sources, and the Soviet forces were given the mobility, rations, and supplies which enabled them to keep up an almost continuous offensive from 1943.

During the first year of the war, about 20 to 25 per cent of the *matériel* procured by the U.S. Army had been assigned or earmarked for the armies of Allied nations.

Lavish equipment

By their own estimates, the U.S. forces in Europe and the Pacific were the most lavishly equipped combatants in the war. Though this caused amazement and some

ridicule by allies and enemy alike, it should be remembered that the land they fought over had either lost or never possessed communications, housing, and public utilities. By bringing their own bath units, pre-fabricated huts, mountains of rations, and vast motor transport pools, U.S. forces enabled the war-ravaged nations of Europe and Asia to employ their resources to re-build their economies as soon as their liberation had been completed.

It was with these considerations in mind that having mastered the U-boat menace, American forces in the United Kingdom built up vast stocks before the invasion of Normandy. By June 1944, 16 million tons of cargo had been shipped across the Atlantic in two years. The choice of Normandy for major landings in Europe was determined by the need to provide a sustained flow of supplies and reinforcements. While other sites might have provided a greater element of surprise, they would not have enabled the Allies to lay P.L.U.T.O., the Pipe Line Under The Ocean, or tow over the "Mulberry" prefabricated harbours.

The forces in the Pacific operated with lines of communication which stretched across the Pacific. Bases existed at Hawaii and were developed in Australia, but there was no easy "cross-Channel life" as from bases in England to the front in Normandy.

The U.S. Navy task forces came near to combining power, mobility, and range with a self-contained supply system. This allowed them to attack and isolate the Japanese island garrisons stuck at the end of vulnerable marine supply lines. When U.S. forces moved in to invade the islands, there was a frantic operation to build up stocks as soon as the troops had gained a footing ashore. Landing ships were loaded so that they could off-load their cargo and turn around in the same day.

Late in the war supply ships would sail direct from the U.S. west coast, by-passing intermediate bases, to forward areas where they would serve as floating warehouses until their cargoes were exhausted.

Ships and aircraft served as the main sources of supply and liaison in the Pacific. In Burma, aircraft became a life-line for the Chinese when the Japanese captured the Burma Road. Beginning in June 1942 the U.S. 10th Air Force flew fuel, ammunition, and stores over "the Hump" the 21,000-foot mountains of the eastern Hima-

layas in south-eastern Tibet. Initially the flow was hardly more than a gesture to the Chinese, but by the last eight months of the operation, aircraft were flying an average of 50,000 tons a month. However, fuel costs in the operation were enormous and air transport remained primarily a means of emergency movement when speed was paramount.

When the Germans had planned their defence of Europe their policy was "Hold the ports and you will hold the coast." It was a sound theory, but was invalidated by the two Mulberry harbours at St. Laurent on "Omaha" Beach and Arromanches on "Gold" Beach.

The German garrison at Cherbourg, however, took care to render the docks unusable before they surrendered. The cranes were blown into the harbour, ships sunk, and finally the water clogged with all the mines available. With other ports along the Channel still held by isolated but determined garrisons, supplies had to be brought from the Mulberries in a continuous stream of trucks whose priority route became known as the "Red Ball Express".

It was a gruelling system which spared

▽ An ambulance on the return trip drives through the village of Loriol in southern France in September 1944. Around the gutted buildings are the remains of a German column smashed on the road, and bulldozed aside by the advancing Americans.
Losses in vehicles through capture and destruction severely strained German logistics, but the armies were retreating towards Germany, shortening the distance between the front line and their main supply dumps.

neither the drivers nor their vehicles. In mid-September major repairs stood at 2,500, and by the end of the month these had risen to 5,750, while the trucks wore out tyres at an average rate of 29,142 a month. In September, 55,059, 8-ply 750 × 20 tyres were used up. By the end of the pursuit period in September, Red Ball had delivered 135,000 tons of supplies to army service areas. These figures, however, were dwarfed later by the "XYZ" operation in 1945, which supported the final drive on Germany.

Despite this system, the mechanised armies sometimes outran their supplies, and like the 3rd Army in the summer of 1944, were brought to a halt with empty fuel tanks.

Vast effort

By the end of World War II "service support" constituted about 45 per cent of the total strength of the U.S. Army. Only three out of every ten soldiers had combat functions, and even within the ranks of a combat division one man in four was classified in the non-combatant group.

Given the distance that supplies had to travel, these figures are not surprising. Winter uniforms, for example, would leave the factory and be sent to a depot. Thence they would go to a port of embarkation, an overseas port, a rear area depot, perhaps then to an intermediate or advanced depot, to a regulating station, to an army-area supply point, to a division or regimental supply point, and finally to the troops.

Often described as a "pipe-line", this system did not in fact provide a steady flow of supplies, but rather stock-piled them as far forward as was safe and practicable. When a major attack was in the offing these stocks would be increased.

In Europe the system developed into a vast complex of depots, traffic regulation points, and railway marshalling yards (which held rolling-stock specially built in the U.S. for operation on continental railways). There were rest areas for the troops, and vehicle repair shops, artillery and tank parks, oil and petrol storage tanks and pipelines, and the offices and headquarters to administer them.

The administration and organisation of this rear-area empire needed a vast array of military departments. Besides transportation, with its subordinate units covering stowage, documentation of ship-

ments, administration of troop and freight movements, and traffic control, there were seven other major service administrative units.

These were:
1. communications;
2. construction, repair, and maintenance facilities;
3. personnel and administration;
4. dissemination of public information;
5. finance and fiscal management;
6. military justice and discipline; and
7. military government.

These services might not appear to be directly connected with the supply of food, equipment, and ammunition to the front, but without them the system would never have operated.

The new science comes of age

Except in the peasant guerrilla armies of the Far East, logistics had ceased to be a haphazard process of living off the land. They had become big business on an international scale, with a department devoted to the study and development of improved methods of man and *matériel* management.

▷ *A "quad .50" anti-aircraft mounting on a half-track vehicle passes through the village of Waldweisse in Lorraine in January 1945. By a strict definition, even anti-aircraft units could be classified as part of the logistic support chain.*
▷▷ *A M10 3-inch Gun Motor Carriage halts near Le Colunvier in southern France, during Operation "Dragoon", as its crew scan the terrain.*

THE HEAVYWEIGHTS

▷ *A Sherman tank with a bulldozer attachment ploughs into a* bocage *hedge in Normandy. The attachment saved the tank from riding up and exposing its thin belly armour to enemy anti-tank weapons.*

▽ *Members of a tank crew of the U.S. 3rd Army make final adjustments to the electrical firing mechanism of the battery of 60 4.5-inch rockets fitted to their Sherman. The rocket unit was disposable after it had been fired. Introduced late in the war, it gave the Sherman an impressive close-support punch.*

◁ At the other end of the armour scale an M8 light armoured car stops near a burned and blasted house in northern Europe. Its crew have strapped packs, sleeping bags, and stores around the turret; and with their own water and fuel, they are a self-contained reconnaissance unit.

▽ An M25 tank transporter recovers a Sherman during an exercise. Capable of carrying 40 tons, the vehicle was 58 feet long and weighed 45 tons. In operational conditions it carried sufficient food for its crew to work independently for four days.

3186

Tributes to artillery have come from generals and commanders since the invention of gunpowder. Encased in armour, and mounted on a cross-country chassis, the gun revolutionised war in the 20th Century.

American armour and artillery were a surprising contrast during most of World War II. Her guns were mobile, accurate, and powerful, but until the introduction of the M26 Pershing her tanks were poor rivals to the heavier German types.

Her guns ranged from the 75-mm pack howitzer, which gave excellent service in the jungle and with airborne forces, to the massive 240-mm howitzer. The 155-mm "Long Tom" and the 8-inch howitzer shared a similar carriage, while the 155-mm howitzer had a surprisingly compact two-wheel carriage.

At the fortified Channel ports, American gunners showed that they could use their guns like the old siege weapons of the Middle Ages. Depressed to their minimum elevation, 155-mm Long Toms fired over open sights at the German positions in Brest and Cherbourg. Later the 240-mm howitzers and the long barrelled 8-inch guns were uncorked against the bunkers of the Sieg-

fried Line.

The limited range and low pay-load of bombers in World War I meant that massive railway guns could be employed in safety behind the front line. In World War II, however, permanent emplacements, and even slow moving railway guns, were at the mercy of enemy bombers. Though the Germans employed some very heavy weapons at Sevastopol' in 1942, they possessed almost total air superiority in the East at that time.

At Corregidor the heavy mortars had no overhead cover and consequently the crews were very vulnerable to enemy fire and aerial attack. The weapons themselves were of such massive construction that many sustained only superficial damage.

Heavy guns, however, were becoming too expensive compared with bombers. Barrel wear, the cost of each shell, and the large numbers of men needed to defend, operate, and supply a heavy gun contrasted unfavourably with the running costs of a B-17, B-24, or B-29.

In the Pacific the main armament on U.S. warships was used against Japanese naval guns emplaced in the defences of Manila. This prompted one officer to say

"Tell Bull Halsey to stop looking for the Jap fleet; it's dug in on Nichols Field."

Though Japanese islands were subject to days of heavy naval bombardment, they were sometimes too small to allow for the satisfactory deployment of large-calibre weapons. The destruction of enemy bunkers fell to the tanks and infantry, or to the cool nerves of a combat engineer with a satchel charge.

Bunker-busting in Europe and the Pacific was a curious contrast. In operations against the Siegfried Line M12 self-propelled 155-mm guns blasted concrete seven feet thick. The best range was about 1,000 to 2,000 yards, where the gun was out of small arms range; some guns, however, were driven to within 300 yards and here it needed only one shot to knock out the position completely.

In the Pacific, 105-mm howitzers were used. First they fired a few rounds with a super-quick fuse to clear away the undergrowth. About ten- to 15-second delay fused shells followed, aimed through the firing slit, and this was enough to destroy the emplacement with its occupants. This drill was also employed with lower calibre weapons like the

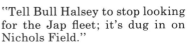

△ ◁ ◁ *A 155-mm gun firing point blank at the St. Malo citadel during the final assault in August 1944. The 155-mm gun, nicknamed "Long Tom", fired 95-pound shells at a rate of 40 rounds an hour. Its 23-foot barrel could be elevated to a maximum of 65 degrees either manually or by means of a fast action hydraulic system.*

◁ *Two 8-inch guns in d'Erezey in Belgium in 1945. The gun could fire a 240-pound shell some ten and a half miles; despite its 14-ton weight it was a very mobile gun.*

△ ◁ *A 155-mm howitzer on a Belgian road near Grandmenil. Like the gun of the same calibre, the howitzer was both mobile and accurate.*

△ *An unusual load for a prime mover: a M4 18-ton high speed tractor, with some tree trunks, passes infantry on the Colmar front. The tractor had a crew of between 9 and 11 and with a built-in stowage compartment for ammunition was used for towing heavy artillery.*

△ Gunners of the 15th Marines manhandle their 105-mm howitzer into a new position. With a muzzle velocity of 1,550 feet per second, it had a range of 11,500 yards. It could fire a wide variety of shells, including H.E., chemical, and leaflet.

▷ The crew of an M7 Gun Motor Carriage take a break at Anzio. The vehicle carried 69 rounds of howitzer ammunition and 300 rounds of .50-inch machine gun ammunition. Its maximum speed of 24 mph gave the Allies mobility and efficient fire-power.

▷▷ The 12-inch mortars of Corregidor, manned by men of the U.S. Coastal Artillery. In static emplacements, with no overhead cover, they fell easy victim to artillery and aerial attack.

7-mm, but here it was less effective.

In armour the Americans came up against tanks that the Germans had designed to combat the superb Soviet models which appeared on the Eastern Front. They found their M4 Shermans were underarmed and thinly armoured; but with greater speed and in larger numbers they could swarm round the lurking Panzers and hit them on the flanks. In the field the crews added timber, and bags, and track shoes to thicken their armour, and later the Sherman was upgunned with a 76-mm gun or a British 17-pounder.

The Sherman chassis was used for a variety of weapons carrying flame-throwers, anti-aircraft guns, field artillery, and as the M10 Tank Destroyer it carried a 3-inch gun.

The tank destroyer was something of a stop-gap measure developed during the war to give armoured units increased hitting power. The M10 first saw action in North Africa, and in one 25-minute skirmish near Bizerta a single T.D. destroyed four German tanks, an 8.8-cm gun, and a number of small combat vehicles, including an armoured car–an impressive record.

Later Patton's 3rd Army claimed that in 231 days of fighting in Germany and France its tank destroyers knocked out 648 German tanks, 211 self-propelled guns, 349 anti-tank guns, 175 artillery pieces, 801 bunkers and pill-boxes, and 1,556 vehicles, which points to the effectiveness of the weapon.

On V.E. Day there were 310 M26 Pershing tanks in Europe; 200 had been issued to the troops but only 20 had seen action. This important vehicle combined a powerful 90-mm gun with a maximum speed of 30 mph and a maximum armour thickness of 102 mm. It was originally hoped that it could take on the German Tiger tank. In 1944 the Pershing was classified as a heavy tank (weighing 41 tons), but by post-war standards it was a medium tank. Despite this, it taught many lessons in tank design which influence fighting vehicle design today.

While hardly a heavyweight at 18 tons, the M24 Chaffee light tank was the culmination of U.S. war-time light tank design. Like the Pershing, it had been developed in the light of combat experience. Compared with the earlier M5 it had well-sloped armour, which compensated for its modest maximum thickness of 38 mm. Its chief recommendation was its 75-mm gun, for earlier light tanks had carried either a machine gun or a small calibre (37-mm) gun.

Chaffees took part in the Rhine crossing and the final advance into Germany, but saw little major action. It was in Korea in

▷ *A 240-mm howitzer is towed up to a firing position by a converted M3A4 tank. It was the largest mobile gun in Italy in 1944.*

▽ *Two of the crew with the 360-lb shell fired by the gun. It had a maximum range of 25,225 yards. On the right of the picture is the cradle for carrying these massive rounds to the breach.*

▷▷ *The breach. The gun fired 30 rounds an hour or one round per minute rapid fire for a maximum of 30 minutes. It could drop its shells a minimum of 8,450 yards from its position.*

▷▷▽ *The gun fires. It weighed 25.5 tons overall, and broke down into barrel and carriage, which were transported separately. It elevated from 15 to 65 degrees and traversed 22.5 degrees.*

3191

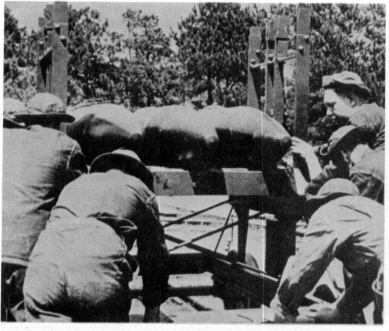

A giant comes out of hybernation: a huge 16-inch coast defence howitzer at Fort Story, Virginia.

△ △ *The gun-crew wheel out three shells for loading.*

△ △▷ *Silk cases, loaded with gun cotton, are pushed into the massive breach.*

△ *The crew turn their backs to the blast as the gun fires out to sea.*

△▷ *The concussion shakes the ground and raises the dust while smoke pours from the gun. Weapons of this size were of diminishing value with the introduction of bombers. The wear on the barrel and the cost of each round fired, about $2,000, meant that no super-heavy static guns were produced by the Allies during the war.*

1950 that the M24 was to be blooded against North Korean T-34/85's. Here, though outgunned, its 35 mph and courageous crews produced a performance which would not normally be expected from a light tank faced with a medium tank.

The M8 armoured car, at 7¾ tons, mounted a 37-mm gun and either a .30-inch or a .50-inch machine gun. It was admired by the British for its cross-country performance. The British gave their vehicles the name "Greyhound". As a reconnaissance vehicle it was ideal with its powerful six-cylinder, 110-bhp Hercules JXD. By the end of the war Ford had built a total of 12,564 M8 armoured cars. The U.S. Army employed them in the same aggressive style that had

typified German light armoured units in their Blitzkrieg heyday. During and after the war these armoured cars were furnished to many other countries in the world.

America had her heavyweights, like the 16-inch coast defence howitzer at Fort Story, Virginia. These guns, however, were left over from another war, and brought out from their "moth balls" at artillery proving grounds. The heavyweights which were produced by World War II might seem modest compared to World War I monsters. Their mobility and fire-power, however, made World War I weapons look like some prehistoric monsters. It is a measure of the quality of the 155-mm gun and the 105-mm howitzer that

they remain in service toda and have featured in many of th small, but no less bloody, wa which have flared up since th end of World War II: career, Indi Pakistan, Israel/the Arab state

American armour reflected th development race which bega with tanks equipped with twi machine guns, and ended wit small forts on tracks mountin 38-cm rocket projectors. Thoug some of her early tanks suffere from poor armour and guns, th tanks and fighting vehicles wit which America ended the wa were some of the best in the world Like her guns they continued t be used after the war in a wid range of operational condition and pointed the way to ne designs and concepts in armoure vehicles.

CHAPTER 184
Air power in the Pacific

▽ *Even in her dying throes, Japan was still capable of striking back at the forces that had driven her back across the Pacific and were now preparing to invade the Japanese homeland: the American "Essex" class fleet carrier* Hancock (ex Ticonderoga) *streams a pall of smoke after being hit by a kamikaze aircraft. It was on April 7, 1945 that the* Hancock *was hit by an aircraft loaded with a 1,000-lb bomb. Seventy-two members of the crew were killed, with another 82 wounded.*
Overleaf: *Carriers of Vice-Admiral Marc Mitscher's command head for Tokyo during the strike that distracted Japanese attention during the Okinawa landings.*

▽ *A Japanese destroyer takes violent evasive action during the Battle of the Bismarck Sea. This was an air-naval battle that took place between March 2 and 4, 1943, when the medium bombers of Major-General Kenney's 5th Air Force attacked a convoy of eight destroyers, taking 7,000 troops to Lae from Rabaul. Seven transports and four destroyers were sunk by the 5th Air Force; a P.T. boat sank the eighth transport. Kenney lost two bombers and three fighters, the Japanese 25 aircraft.*

Japan's surprise attack on Pearl Harbor in 1941 was the first of several major carrier operations which were to shape the course of the war in the Pacific. In a theatre which contained a vastly larger proportion of sea to land, many targets were out of range of land-based aircraft and so the fighter-bombers were ferried to them by carriers.

Just as in Europe rival air forces would attempt to knock out enemy airfields, so too, in the Pacific, carriers became a primary target.

Japan committed just over half her front line carrier force to the assault on Pearl Harbor. *Akagi, Kaga, Shokaku, Zuikaku, Soryu,* and *Hiryu* launched 360 torpedo, horizontal, high-level, and dive-bombers and fighters in an attack which, though it crippled the American Pacific Fleet, still left afloat its cruisers and carriers. Unburdened by the slower battleships, these vessels became the key elements of the task force fleets which ranged through the Pacific later in the War.

Pearl Harbor, however, was reduced to a scrapyard of crippled or capsized battleships. Of the eight present, three were sunk, one capsized, and the remainder seriously damaged. Three light cruisers.

three destroyers, and other vessels were sunk or seriously damaged. On land, of 231 Army aircraft only 166 remained intact or repairable, and only 54 out of the Navy's 250 were usable. More than 3,000 Navy and Marine officers and men were killed, and the Army lost 226 men.

Heavy as these losses were, the Japanese had failed to hit the major repair facilities and the oil tank farm, and so they had not deprived the remaining ships of their mobility. Given that they were risking all, in what the world saw as a treacherous attack, the Japanese did not show the determination in the attack that was to

characterise their later operations. They spent just under two hours over the base and lost 28 planes. If they had spent longer in the area, they might have caught the U.S. carrier *Enterprise*, which was returning from Wake. With a three to one advantage in aircraft, they could have sunk her at sea, where she would have been lost for good.

Finally, the attack precipitated the Americans into a war that they had been approaching with a careful rearmament policy. By 1943 their "Essex" class carriers, which had been authorised in 1940, were in action south-west of Pearl Harbor.

The accusation that the Japanese could only score quick victories when they had carefully rehearsed their operations in peace-time is partly true. While their attacks on Pearl Harbor, and operations in the Philippines and Malaya, had been preceded by training either on scale models, or on similar terrain, the sinking of the *Prince of Wales* and the *Repulse* demonstrated flexibility and prompt reactions to a favourable situation.

In an assault which lasted about an hour, land-based bombers and torpedo-bombers from Indo-China attacked and sank the two unescorted warships on December 10, 1941. This destruction of capital ships at sea by air attack shocked the British Admiralty, but was the first use of a weapon which would return to plague the Japanese.

Between April 2 and 8, 1942, a Japanese task force spread further panic by sailing into the Indian Ocean and attacking the British base at Ceylon, sinking two cruisers, a destroyer, and the old aircraft-carrier *Hermes*.

However, though they downed the British fighters and torpedo aircraft, their carriers lost a number of aircraft, which affected the forces they could muster at the battle of the Coral Sea.

An unusual and significant sea-borne air operation was launched off the Japanese coast on April 18, 1942. The Doolittle Raid, besides being a boost to American morale, prompted the Japanese high command to expand eastwards to Midway island. It was this operation which led to the American victory at the battle of Midway.

Coral Sea, however, was the first carrier battle in history, and though both sides suffered losses (with a slight tactical advantage going to the Japanese), it marked the end of their victorious expansion. In the battle on May 7 and 8, 1942 the

continued on page 3202

▽ ◁ *A Grumman Avenger circles above a Japanese destroyer off Truk. As a distraction during the Marshalls operation, Mitscher launched a major strike against Truk on February 17-19, 1944. Although Admiral Koga managed to save the Combined Fleet by ordering it to fan out from the island, the Americans caught 50 merchantmen and 359 aircraft at Truk. By mid-day, 200,000 tons of shipping and 275 aircraft had been destroyed, for the loss of 17 aircraft to the Americans.*

△ *A Japanese destroyer begins a turn to port in an effort to evade the attentions of the North American B-25 Mitchell lining itself up for its final run-in over Ormoc Bay. This was part of the American plan to prevent the Japanese landing reinforcements on the west coast of Leyte in the first stage of the Philippines' campaign late in 1944.*

◁ and ▷ *A Japanese destroyer under air attack by machines of the 5th Air Force off Kavieng in April 1944.*
▽ *A Japanese light cruiser sinks in the South China Sea after receiving the attentions of aircraft from Rear-Admiral John S. McCain's carrier task group.*

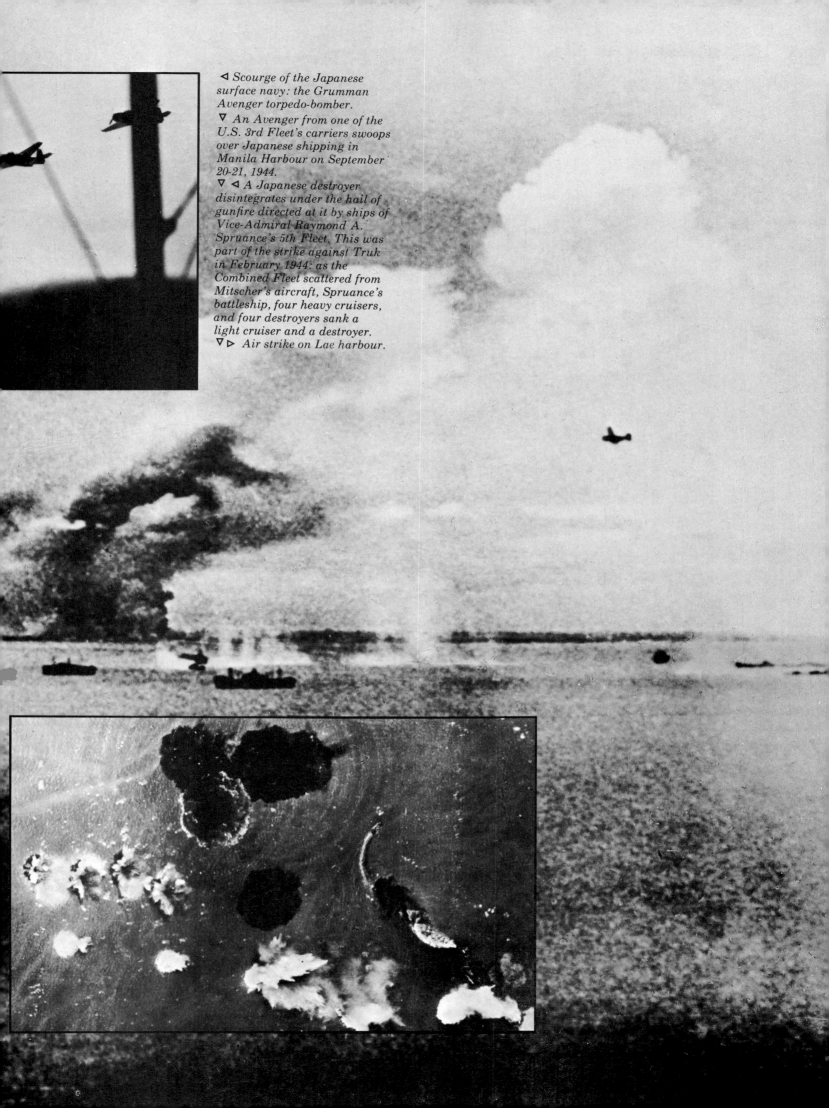

◁ Scourge of the Japanese
surface navy: the Grumman
Avenger torpedo-bomber.
▽ An Avenger from one of the
U.S. 3rd Fleet's carriers swoops
over Japanese shipping in
Manila Harbour on September
20-21, 1944.
▽ ◁ A Japanese destroyer
disintegrates under the hail of
gunfire directed at it by ships of
Vice-Admiral Raymond A.
Spruance's 5th Fleet. This was
part of the strike against Truk
in February 1944: as the
Combined Fleet scattered from
Mitscher's aircraft, Spruance's
battleship, four heavy cruisers,
and four destroyers sank a
light cruiser and a destroyer.
▽ ▷ Air strike on Lae harbour.

continued from page 3197

11,000-ton *Shoho* was sunk by the Americans, who lost the 33,000-ton *Lexington*.

The indisputable victory came a month later, and again it a was a carrier battle. At Midway between June 4 and 6, 1942, the Japanese lost the *Akagi*, *Kaga*, and *Soryu*, and then the *Hiryu*. The first three were lost in a curious reversal of the aerial tactics of that period: instead of the dive-bombers drawing the A.A. fire as the torpedo-bombers slipped in low over the waves, it was the massacre of the low-level attackers which allowed the dive-bombers to strike. Though the Americans lost the

Yorktown, the Japanese had suffered a crippling blow from which they would never recover.

In the autumn of 1943, the 5th Fleet, as it became known in 1944, began to strangle the Japanese supply routes to their isolated island garrisons. The fleet had a formidable carrier arm: six fleet, five light, and eight escort carriers. At its head was the Fast Carrier Task Force of four task groups, each containing two fleet and two light carriers. In addition there were land-based units from the Army, Navy, and Marines which were used for advanced photo-reconnaissance and bombing missions and for operations ashore when an airfield had been captured.

Supporting and providing the logistical management was the Service Force. Its ships were mobile bases for repair and re-supply, and from refuelling at sea it expanded to a full replenishment service that enabled the carriers to stay up front for weeks at a time. By 1945 the system operated so that every day one of the four carrier task groups withdrew from the task force to be resupplied. The replenishment group was itself rotated on station.

In February 1944 Admiral Mitscher's carrier force attacked the Japanese naval base at Truk. By noon on the 17th they had

▽ *Bombs explode around a Japanese merchantman trying to escape from Eniwetok in February 1944.*
▽ ▽ *A Japanese warship* en route *from Singapore to Japan comes in for some close attention from a B-29 Superfortress flown, at very low level, by Lieutenant George R. Schmidt of Goodling, Idaho.*

sunk 200,000 tons of shipping and destroyed 275 aircraft. No attempt was made to occupy the base and it was left to die, slowly starved of the supplies which had gone down in the shipping in the harbour.

The task forces could range through Japanese-held islands, attacking their shipping and airfields, or concentrate for the preparatory softening-up before an invasion. At Leyte and other islands they stood by as floating air support while landing grounds were built or redeveloped.

The Battle of the Philippine Sea, between June 19 and 21, 1944, demonstrated

◁ *A Japanese merchantman, about to meet its end in Ormoc Bay. On this occasion, three merchantmen and six escorts were sunk.*
▽ *Anti-shipping strike off Eniwetok.*
▽▽ *Japanese shipping under air attack during the U.S. 3rd Fleet's strike on Manila harbour on September 20-21, 1944.*

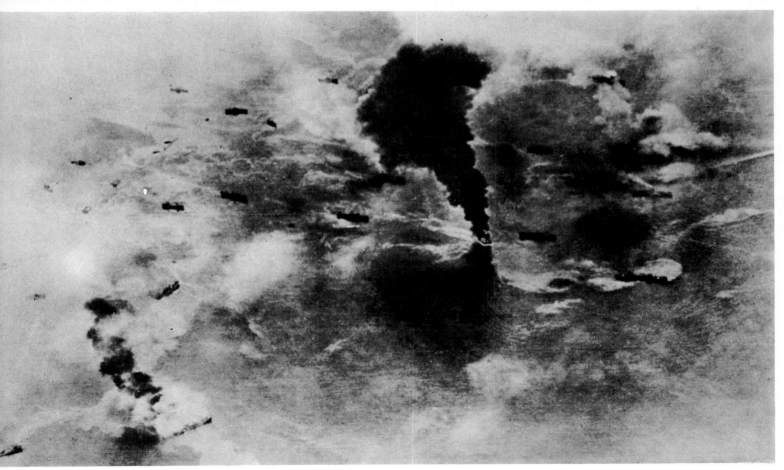

what well-handled carriers with radar-vectored fighters can do under bold and mature leadership. Of the 430 Japanese aircraft involved, 330 were shot down in what became known as "the Great Marianas Turkey Shoot". American submarines torpedoed the *Taiho* and the *Shokaku*, and in air attacks the Japanese lost a further two carriers, and with them the valuable air crews.

In a daring strike in the late afternoon of the 20th Mitscher launched 216 aircraft which sank two oil tankers and another carrier. Twenty planes were lost and in the gathering dusk Mitscher lit up his carriers and fired star shell to guide his pilots home. After destroyers had searched the attack approach area in the morning, the fleet recovered 160 of the 209 airmen used in the strike. The planes lost when the pilots ditched in the night were of little value compared with the men whose combat experience was irreplaceable.

In the Battle of Leyte Gulf, air power again demonstrated that a capital ship without fighter protection was useful only as target practice once it had been located

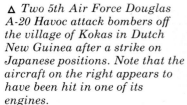
△ *Two 5th Air Force Douglas A-20 Havoc attack bombers off the village of Kokas in Dutch New Guinea after a strike on Japanese positions. Note that the aircraft on the right appears to have been hit in one of its engines.*
▷ *5th Air Force aircrew after a mission to Madang. The man with the camera is a Life magazine correspondent.*
▷ ▷ *Incendiary raid by the 5th Air Force on Rabaul airfield. It was from here, in New Britain, and Lae in New Guinea that the Japanese operated aircraft in support of their troops in the Solomons and New Guinea areas.*
Overleaf: *A "South Dakota" class battleship off Okinawa.*

by the enemy. This time, however, it was the Japanese who learned the lesson. On October 24, 1944, the massive 64,200-ton battleship *Musashi* was sunk after two days of aerial attack by Mitscher's Task Force 38. It took 19 torpedoes and 17 bombs, delivered in 250 sorties, to sink the heavily-armoured monster.

The Americans did not escape undamaged from the battle. The light carrier *Princeton* was hit by a lone Japanese bomber whose 550-lb bomb penetrated the flight deck and set fire to aircraft fuel. Rent by internal explosions, the blazing hulk was later sunk by the Americans.

An attack as novel as it was terrifying sank the light carrier *St Lo* on October 25. Nine *kamikaze* aircraft in one of the first attacks of the war screamed down to sink the vessel and damage others.

Early the following year the Japanese demonstrated a capacity for *kamikaze* operations on a gigantic scale. The sister ship of the *Musashi*, the *Yamato*, was loaded with ammunition and enough fuel for a one-way trip to the invasion fleet at Okinawa. On April 7, 1945 she was met by aircraft from Mitscher's carriers and

repeatedly attacked. After four hours of constant assault, in which she took ten torpedoes and five bombs, she slid under with some 2,488 officers and men on board.

Had the Japanese concentrated their remaining air power in defending the battleship, she might have reached the invasion fleet and, with the 42,000-yard range of her nine 18.1-inch guns, she could have stood off and bombarded, out of range of the U.S. warships. As it was, the aircraft were dissipated in *kamikaze* attacks, and the Americans lost only 15 aircraft and 84 seamen and pilots in what was the last fling of the Japanese navy.

Though the Japanese had been operating on interior lines, by the spring of 1944 the Americans had the initiative following the Battle of the Philippine Sea. The lighter, less complex and less heavily armoured

△ ◁ *An L.C.V.(P.) begins to lay a smokescreen round an L.S.T. in an effort to shield it from the attentions of the* kamikazes *off Okinawa.*
◁ *The "Essex" class fleet carrier* Ticonderoga, *badly damaged by* kamikazes *off Formosa on January 21, 1945.*
▷ *The pattern of naval air war in the Far East: part of a fast carrier group under air attack.*
▽ ◁ *The crew of an American aircraft-carrier cheers as a* kamikaze, *shot down by its guns, crashes into the sea.*

aircraft of the Imperial Army and Navy had about a 200- to 300-mile range advantage over the Americans. But their pilots were badly trained, for Japan did not have sufficient fuel for flying training after the attacks on her tankers off Borneo by U.S. submarines.

Task Force 58, under Spruance, operated in five sections which were no more than 15 miles apart, and so they could concentrate or be mutually supporting. The Japanese had not learned the value of this lesson and spread their forces in five groups which were 100 miles apart, and so attacks on the lead units could not be beaten off by forces in the main body.

By 1945 American carrier forces were operating off the home islands of Japan and supplementing the work of the B-29's with strategic attacks on naval bases, airfields, and military industrial targets. These operations were like the attacks launched against occupied Europe from British airfields, with the difference that the fighter-bombers were sea, rather than

land, based.

The analogy of Britain as the unsinkable aircraft carrier, or carriers as floating islands, can be extended to the employment of radar. Just as in the Battle of Britain radar gave early warning of German attacks, so too the Americans used picket destroyers with radar to detect Japanese attacks. American aircraft could be launched to attack the Japanese, to clear the decks for emergency landings, and to remove these soft-skinned targets from damage by blast or bomb or shell fragments.

Though the aircraft could be removed from the target area, the carriers themselves remained vulnerable. Both U.S. and Japanese vessels were built with unarmoured decks, unlike their British counterparts. While this gave them a greater aircraft capacity and slightly higher speed, the British ships could remain in action after they had been hit by a *kamikaze*, but many American carriers were severely damaged when Japanese bombs or aircraft ploughed through the deck to explode in the hangars and storage areas. Japanese flight decks, too, were an easy target for U.S. dive-bombers, whose bombs could penetrate the timber decks and burst in the ship's vitals.

The Japanese froze aircraft design too early in the war and though they made attempts to make up the ground lost to the more modern American types that began to appear in 1943 and 1944, fuel restrictions hampered their training and development programme.

The aircraft with which they began the war were adequate for their rôles, and in the case of the A6M Zero more than a match for Allied fighters. The Allies were surprised not only by the quality of the aircraft, but also by the competence of the pilots. This belief that the Japanese were incapable of original design or efficient tactics was the more reprehensible as Claire Chennault had met them over China and warned the Americans, who had blithely ignored the information.

The types with which the Japanese began and fought much of the war were the Zero, the Aichi D3A2 dive-bomber, and the Nakajima B5N2 torpedo-bomber. The Zero, a fast and manoeuvrable fighter,

◁ *Part of an American carrier group operating between the Marshalls and the Gilberts. This was part of a sweep by Halsey with the* Enterprise *and* Yorktown *on February 1, 1942, which helped to set the pattern for later operations.*

3211

▷ *The carrier* Hancock *in flames after being hit first by a kamikaze's bomb, then by the* kamikaze *itself. This happened at 1212 on April 7, 1945. By 1230 the fires were under control and by 1300 they were all but out. By 1630 she could recover her aircraft and even operate them on an emergency basis.*
▷▷ *The carrier* Franklin *after being hit by a kamikaze.*
▽ Kamikaze *damage off Mindoro: a destroyer pumps water onto the stricken ships as smaller vessels edge in to take off the supplies loaded on the deck.*
▽▷ *The less successful early days: the "Saratoga" class carrier* Lexington *succumbs to Japanese torpedoes during the Battle of the Coral Sea on May 8, 1942.*

mounted two cannons and machine guns, and later models could reach 351 mph.

The Aichi "Val" was Japan's first all-metal low-wing monoplane dive-bomber. It carried up to 816 lbs of bombs and in the hands of a skilled pilot was a very efficient weapon. Indeed, after dropping its bombs it could engage enemy fighters, being strongly built.

The Nakajima "Kate", though vulnerable to fighter attack, was the torpedo-bomber used at Pearl Harbor. It was relegated to anti-submarine duties later in the war and replaced by the Nakajima B6N2 *Tenzan* "Jill".

American aircraft development made up the deficiencies made apparent at the beginning of the war, and their types were used by the British and French during and after the war.

The tubby Grumman F4F Wildcat was the U.S. Navy's standard single-seat fighter when the U.S. entered the war. It could carry two 100-lb bombs and was armed with four .5-inch machine guns. Outnumbered in the early days, Wildcats were still able to give a good performance and at the end of the 1941-1943 period they had destroyed 905 enemy aircraft for the loss of 178 machines. They had already served with distinction in the Royal Navy. Later marks incorporated improvements suggested by both U.S. and Royal Navy pilots.

The Grumman F6F Hellcat was a classic example of the speed and efficiency of American war production, which overwhelmed Japan and Germany. The first F6F-3 flew on July 30, 1942 and the first planes were assigned to the *Essex* on January 16, 1943. A mere 18 months after the prototype's first flight they were used in an attack on Marcus Island, flying from the *Yorktown*. Armed with six .5-inch machine guns, plus two 1,000-lb bombs or six 5-inch rockets, the F6F-5 had a maximum speed of 386 mph. It was supplemented rather than replaced by the Vought F4U Corsair.

The Vought Corsair was at the time of its appearance the most powerful naval fighter ever built. The Japanese came to know it as the "Whistling Death", and this type destroyed well over 2,000 enemy aircraft by the end of the war. The F4U-4 had a maximum speed of 446 mph and an armament of six .5-inch machine guns. It could carry two 1,000-lb bombs or eight 5-inch rockets. Though the U.S. Navy at first considered the Corsair to be unsuitable for carrier use, the Royal Navy used

continued on page 3218

▽ *A Vought-Sikorsky OS2U-3 Kingfisher reconnaissance aircraft about to take off for a scouting mission over Okinawa. After being launched from the catapult on the battleship's stern, the plane would have to land on the water alongside and be lifted back on board by crane.*

▷ *A pilotless drone, basically a Grumman Hellcat fighter, is catapulted from the carrier Shangri-La.*

▽ *Avengers on board the escort carrier Card, the most successful submarine killer of the war.*

▽ ▷ *A Hellcat climbs over the bows of its carrier after take-off. Note the droppable fuel tank under the belly.*

▽ ▷ ▷ *An Avenger torpedo-bomber ditched in the Pacific. This occurred when the machine banked at low level and the wing-tip hit the water. The crew are preparing to inflate their life-raft.*

continued from page 3213

it to provide air cover for the torpedo-bombers launched from the *Victorious* against the *Tirpitz* on April 3, 1944. Nine months after the type had been used successfully by the Royal Navy, the U.S. Navy accepted it for ship-board operations. It was the last piston-engined fighter to be built in the U.S.A.

The Douglas SBD Dauntless dive-bomber was already obsolescent by the time of Pearl Harbor. In the absence of other aircraft of that type it served with distinction in the early years, and its rugged design gave it the lowest loss rate of any other carrier-borne aircraft in the U.S. Pacific Fleet. It could carry two 100-lb, one 500-lb, or one 1,000-lb bomb, or two depth charges. It had a maximum speed of 252 mph and mounted two .5- and two .3-inch machine guns.

It was supplemented, but not fully replaced, by the Curtiss SB2C Helldiver, which first saw action on November 11, 1943. This carried a torpedo or up to 1,000 lbs of bombs internally and was armed with two 20-mm cannon and one .5-inch machine gun.

The Grumman TBF Avenger, with a loaded weight of 13,667 lbs and wing span of 54 feet 2 inches, was one of the largest carrier aircraft of its time. It was one of the few that could carry a 22-inch torpedo internally, and with its power-operated turret it had a formidable armament including three .5- and two .3-inch machine guns.

Two Japanese aircraft which featured in naval operations, though they were not carrier based, merit attention. The Mitsubishi G4M "Betty" bomber and the Yokosuka MXY-7 *Okha* "Baka" piloted flying bomb.

The Betty, with the G3M2 "Nell", was used in the attack on the *Prince of Wales* and the *Repulse*. The pilots pressed home their bombing attacks and dropped their torpedoes so that though the ships could comb one strike, they turned into the tracks of the other torpedoes.

A twin-engined bomber, the Betty could carry up to 2,200 lbs of bombs or one 1,764-lb torpedo. With a range of 2,262 miles, the aircraft which attacked the *Prince of Wales* and *Repulse* were almost at the end of their operational radius.

The *Okha* was the "logical" development of the *kamikaze* tactics which reflected the deterioration in Japanese military thought.

With three solid-fuel rocket motors and a warhead of 2,645 lbs of explosive, the

△ *Narrow escape for an "Independence" class light carrier as a* kamikaze *crashes into her wake.*
△▷ *L.S.T.s of the Green Island invasion force, accompanied by an armed auxiliary fleet tug, change course at the beginning of a zig-zag intended to avoid interception by submarines and aircraft.*
▽ *American ships put up a smokescreen to protect the Leyte invasion force.*

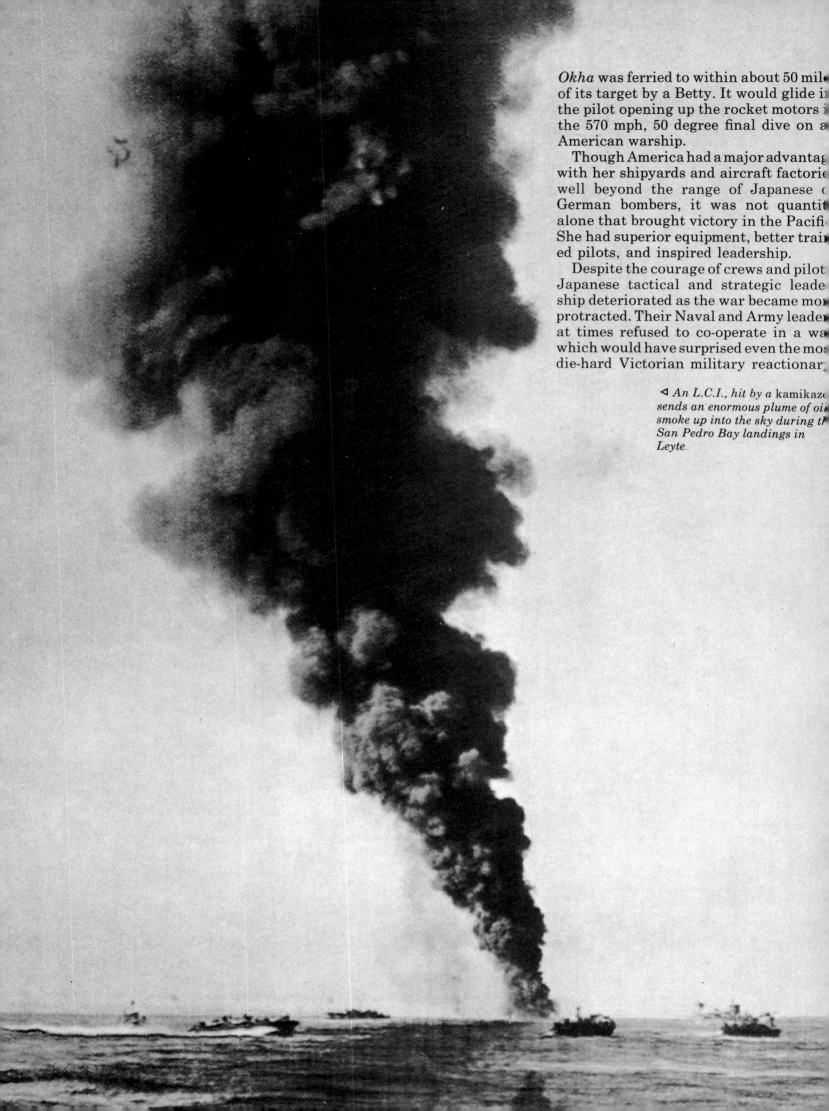

Okha was ferried to within about 50 mil⟨es⟩ of its target by a Betty. It would glide i⟨n⟩ the pilot opening up the rocket motors i⟨n⟩ the 570 mph, 50 degree final dive on a⟨n⟩ American warship.

Though America had a major advantag⟨e⟩ with her shipyards and aircraft factorie⟨s⟩ well beyond the range of Japanese ⟨or⟩ German bombers, it was not quantit⟨y⟩ alone that brought victory in the Pacifi⟨c⟩ She had superior equipment, better trai⟨n⟩ed pilots, and inspired leadership.

Despite the courage of crews and pilot⟨s⟩ Japanese tactical and strategic leade⟨r⟩ship deteriorated as the war became mo⟨re⟩ protracted. Their Naval and Army leade⟨rs⟩ at times refused to co-operate in a wa⟨y⟩ which would have surprised even the mos⟨t⟩ die-hard Victorian military reactionar⟨y⟩

◁ *An L.C.I., hit by a kamikaze* *sends an enormous plume of oi⟨ly⟩* *smoke up into the sky during th⟨e⟩* *San Pedro Bay landings in* *Leyte.*